SECRET CITY OF DURHAM

Derek Dodds

AMBERLEY

First published 2016

Amberley Publishing
The Hill, Stroud
Gloucestershire, GL5 4EP

www.amberley-books.com

Copyright © Derek Dodds, 2016

The right of Derek Dodds to be identified as the
Author of this work has been asserted in accordance
with the Copyrights, Designs and Patents Act 1988.

ISBN 978 1 4456 4696 1 (print)
ISBN 978 1 4456 4697 8 (ebook)

British Library Cataloguing in Publication Data.
A catalogue record for this book is available from the
British Library.

Origination by Amberley Publishing.
Printed in Great Britain.

Contents

	Introduction	6
1.	'A City ... Fine and Faire'	
	(Quoted in *A Sketch of Durham*, E. J. Morton, 1885)	8
2.	All's Well	10
3.	Another Durham	12
4.	Buried Gates and Broken Walls	14
5.	Busy Bee	17
6.	Castle in the Sky	19
7.	Crossing the Water	22
8.	Durham Behind Bars	24
9.	Girl Power	27
10.	Going Underground	29
11.	Grave Matters	32
12.	The Great, the Good and the Forgotten	34
13.	Hidden Hall	37
14.	In and Out	40
15.	Let There be Light (and Indoor Plumbing)	42
16.	Little, Large and Tall	45
17.	Men of Many Parts	48
18.	Moonfleet Man	50
19.	Mr Henderson's Hall	53
20.	Music Men	56
21.	Name Game	58
22.	Open and Shut	60
23.	Pointing the Way	62
24.	Prison Without Cells	64
25.	School's Out	66
26.	Secret Services	68
27.	Secret Stones	70
28.	Shopping Days	72
29.	Sign of the Cross	74
30.	Take a Letter	76
31.	Take a Seat	78
32.	'The Play's the Thing' (*Hamlet* – Act 2)	80
33.	The Prince and the Pitman	82
34.	Up and Down	84
35.	Valley of Secrets	86
36.	Water Walks	88
37.	Where's the Whale?	90
38.	Last Look	92
	Bibliography	94
	Acknowledgements	95

Map Key (Source – OpenStreetMap)

1. Durham Cathedral
2. Durham Castle
3. Palace Green
4. Divinity House
5. Windy Gap
6. Owengate
7. Dun Cow Lane
8. Assembly Rooms
9. St Mary-le-Bow
10. Bow Lane
11. St Mary-the-Less
12. South Bailey
13. Prebends' Bridge
14. Watergate
15. Prebends' Walk
16. Dark Entry
17. St Chad's
18. North Bailey
19. Drury Lane
20. Magdalene Steps
21. Saddler Street
22. Fearon's Walk
23. Elvet Bridge
24. Silver Street
25. Market Place
26. Framwellgate Bridge
27. Cuthbert's Well
28. Broken Walls
29. Town Hall / Indoor market
30. St Nicholas
31. Walkergate / City Theatre
32. Gala Theatre
33. Claypath
34. Congregationalist Church and Chapel
35. Quaker Cemetery
36. St Antony's Priory
37. Tinklers' Lane
38. Providence Row
39. St Nicholas Cemetery
40. Site of Penitentiary
41. The Chains
42. Kepier Wood
43. Gilesgate
44. Silverlink Bridge
45. Pelaw Wood
46. Old Durham
47. Maiden Castle Bridge
48. To Houghall Old Pit
49. Old Elvet
50. Old Shire Hall
51. H.M. Prison Durham
52. New Elvet
53. St Oswald's
54. Stockton Road Cemetery
55. Charley's Cross
56. Quarryheads Lane
57. St Mary's College
58. Elvet Hill Cemetery
59. Observatory
60. Neville's Cross Monument
61. Redhills Lane
62. St Bede's Cemetery and Chapel
63. Maiden's Bower
64. Flass Vale
65. Miners' Hall
66. Viaduct
67. North Road
68. Obelisk
69. Wharton Park
70. Tenter Terrace
71. Sutton Street
72. Hawthorn Terrace
73. Durham School
74. The Grove
75. Pimlico
76. South Street
77. Millburngate
78. Crossgate
79. St Helen's Well
80. St Margaret's of Antioch
81. Allergate
82. Fram Well Head
83. Crook Hall
84. To Framwellgate Old Pit

Introduction

'People are always looking for something, and it's right there under their noses.'
Travels Through an Unwrecked Landscape, Candida Lycett Green.

What more can be said about the city of Durham? This marvellous place is one of England's most glittering gems. Castle and cathedral crown a rocky peninsula high above the encircling River Wear, as the buildings below seem to snuggle closer for comfort and protection. Over the centuries, since footsore monks established a resting place for the body of their patriarch St Cuthbert at Durham, its dramatic history and natural beauty has inspired numerous authors and artists. From medieval chroniclers down to the present-day crop of authoritative writers and photographers, Durham has been thoroughly discussed and dissected. This book is indebted to their scholarship and craft but is far from a detailed history; neither is it a city insider's account of this famed location (although I am a native of the 'Land of the Prince Bishops', as County Durham has been christened by the local Tourist Board). Instead it is a kaleidoscope of observations and impressions, springing from regular visits to the city over many years. Like the pilgrims of old, I have followed the winding street pattern, hardly altered since medieval times, which today channels tourists through narrow Owengate into the wide Palace Green and the castle and cathedral beyond. But as visitors converge on these architectural icons, how many realise that hefty gates and walls guarding the citadel would once have barred their way? Traces of them remain and discovering them, if you know where to look, is well worth the effort. Fragments, curios and architectural bric-a-brac like this, unnoticed and ignored, form the theme of this book; their unexpected secrets play small yet telling parts in the Durham story.

Durham's ancient core is relatively compact and can be walked around with ease. Most of my tours tend to end in the cool interior of the cathedral, referred to in 1626 by Robert Hegge as 'this sumptuous church'. Invariably I am drawn along the south aisle towards the Chapel of the Nine Altars and St Cuthbert's tomb. After pausing at the shrine to imagine its pre-Reformation splendour, I usually stop and gaze at the wood sculptures of Durham artist Fenwick Lawson. They are often bathed in tinted light from the stained glass above or glimmer in the afternoon semi-darkness. Carved from elm and beech wood, his compelling work swells with powerful spirituality.

Over half a century ago, as a young teacher, Fenwick was dismayed by one of his student's careless attempts at drawing. Taking the reluctant pupil to an open window, he urged him to look carefully at the amazing world surrounding him. The boy, of course, was me, and although most lessons were soon forgotten, that one has lasted well. Perhaps the purpose of what follows in these pages is to pass this advice on. Visitors to the fabled city of Durham should look longer and harder, and when they return they may see and understand even more.

Peninsula and Framwellgate Bridge.

Owengate to Palace Green.

Once known as Queen Street, Owengate is notable for a nineteenth-century mock-Tudor almshouse at No. 7, now a visitor centre. It contains five fireplaces but there are no chimneys to be seen. After entering the cathedral by the north door, notice the empty recess on the first nave column. Holy water basins or 'stoups' were torn from many church walls during the Reformation.

An unexpected vista of Durham Cathedral appears over the allotments on Margery Place. Appropriately enough, the area was once an orchard and the site of a quarry which may well have provided stone for the great building projects nearby. 'Margery' is probably derived from the adjacent church of St Margaret's of Antioch. The delightful twelfth-century St Margaret's can be reached from a quiet footpath on Grape Lane and the building itself contains a memorial slab to Durham's 'rags to riches' mayor, Sir John Duck. More easily missed is a puzzling medieval carving high on a nave pillar – is it man or beast?

1. 'A City ... Fine and Faire'
(Quoted in *A Sketch of Durham,*
E. J. Morton, 1885)

Although there is some evidence of earlier occupation, Durham City owes its foundation to the arrival of Cuthbert's religious community in 995. Driven first from Lindisfarne in 875, then Chester-le-Street and Ripon by the Viking threat, they settled on 'Dunholm' – the wooded 'hill island' that became Durham. Within a few years a substantial church had been built around the acclaimed northern saint's coffin and a tradition of pilgrimage was established, one that proved hard to break. Even after the Norman Conquest, Cuthbert's spiritual magnetism continued to grow and was celebrated by the construction of a new cathedral that was towering over the peninsula by the early twelfth century. A stone castle was built opposite and ramshackle dwellings in the space between were cleared away to create 'Place' or, as it's now known, 'Palace' Green.

Wealth and prestige flowed from Cuthbert's shrine and led to the establishment of a unique religious and political institution with Durham at its heart. Durham became a palatinate, a semi-independent county appointed by Norman kings, aware of the influence of the Cuthbert cult and eager to turn the region into a defensive buffer against the Scottish threat. Bishops of Durham became 'Princes' indeed because of the extraordinary powers they were granted to ensure this.

In the medieval period these 'Prince Bishops' certainly left their architectural mark, not just on the castle and cathedral but also in other distinctive buildings which complemented them. From the time of Bishop Bek onwards, they also left their armorials – decorative emblems which later influenced municipal insignia. Today shields and full coats of arms are scattered liberally around the city, some unnoticed against more eye-catching façades – around the Town Hall balcony for example, or almost out of sight on the edge of the Tudor-style window above. Only embellishments perhaps, but they are footnotes of history, sometimes instructive and always entertaining to find. See how many you can spot in an hour.

In 1639, a visitor to Durham, impressed by the number of gentry he found there, called the growing town 'the London (as it were) of those north parts' but others complained about cramped and congested streets. At that time, Durham was still a medieval walled city and existing structures were being built over in an attempt to overcome the peninsula's challenging topography.

Beyond the walls and gates, Durham's five old boroughs also began to expand. Through the Victorian period and into the twentieth century the city had its share of pollution and poor housing, although it escaped the worst industrial blight. Great improvements were made, however, and new developments have been created to meet modern demands for road systems and shopping centres. Durham's vigorous conservation lobby has not approved of them all, but in these materialistic and often hectic times, the city thankfully remains as a much-needed source of mystery and inspiration.

Above left: Bishop Cosin's Insignia.

Above right: Guild Hall Balcony.

Right: Barrington's coat of arms.

Every Bishop of Durham's coat of arms clearly illustrates their lofty status. Each contains their individual heraldic devices but prominent in all of them is a ducal coronet and mitre, which only the Prince Bishops were privileged to display.

2. All's Well

Before Victorian ingenuity provided Durham with the first modern water supply in 1849, the city depended heavily on its surrounding wells. Many of them only appear on old street maps and probably would require the skills of a water diviner to find them now, but others have survived, even though some are dried up ruins, or vandalised and barely recognisable. Yet they once played a crucial, if largely forgotten, part in Durham's history, and are reminders of a time when life's everyday essentials could not be taken for granted.

Several brooks once flowed freely into the river around Durham's meandering river gorge, but to overcome the area's geological makeup of sandstone, shale and coal measures, early castle dwellers on top of the peninsula sometimes had to dig deep to reach a water table. In 1904, a castle well 4 feet wide and around 100 feet deep was rediscovered in the courtyard facing the castle's Great Hall. Similarly, a few years earlier the cathedral gave up one secret among many when excavations at the base of the building's west end revealed a water source which seems to be linked to the nearby Galilee and St Cuthbert's wells. Often completely unnoticed, both can be reached from the riverside paths. A truncated archway and ordinary metal grate obscures the Galilee Well, while Cuthbert's, a short distance away to the north and more impressive, is often made almost completely invisible by the foliage allowed to obstruct it. Therefore, winter visits are recommended, but care must be taken with the often slippery climb to the well head from the lower riverside path.

Another well associated with the great northern saints is concealed on the river's opposite bank in the shadow of St Oswald's Church, which some believe has origins far older than Durham Cathedral. The elusive St Oswald's Well lies on the steep river slope just below the churchyard in New Elvet. Nineteenth-century vandalism destroyed its arcaded surround and it now appears as nothing more than a shallow natural cavern in the sandstone cliff face. But cold water that bubbled from so-called 'holy wells' such as this was once commonly believed to quench the thirst and to heal the body and soul.

Many other wells were scattered around the riverside districts, particularly on to the north-west side of the river around Crossgate. Most important among them was the Fram Well, now found down a side road near the medieval Crook Hall. What remains of the well head has been shunted around over the years to avoid Durham's network of new roads, a sad epitaph for a spring which was once piped into the marketplace, providing a major public supply for three centuries.

Mid-nineteenth-century Ordnance Survey maps of the Crossgate area show a further group of wells, six at the foot of South Street and one at the top named the South Street Well, which some writers call St Mary's Well. Water still collects around this obscure rocky outcrop near Prebend's Bridge, but it attracts little attention today.

However, just as intriguing, though now buried underground, is the neighbouring St Helen's Well, known from at least 1418. An exhilarating (or perhaps breathless) walk up

South Street's hill is always rewarded with a picture-postcard view of the cathedral. But before setting off, consider for a moment the contemporary architecture on your left. Remarkably, and like those before it, the latest of a series of buildings here has respected the heritage and retained the name of this ancient site. What was a medieval 'vennel' or passageway to St Mary's Well is acknowledged by an opening into the modern housing development.

South Street Well.

Cuthbert's Well.

Now almost indecipherable, a dedication on St Cuthbert's Well actually reads 1696. This time marked the onset of riverbank 'prettification'. Before then, slopes below the castle were deliberately kept clear of vegetation for reasons of military defence. Over the next century, plantations began to appear, creating the romantic perspectives familiar today. The riverside wells played their part in this and while St Cuthbert's and St Oswald's were still visited and exploited for their popular appeal, others were refashioned to appear as natural features and talking points in a dramatic landscape.

3. Another Durham

Old Durham lives up to its name; it is an obscure little place with a history as ancient as the peninsula it quietly faces from across the Wear. A mile east of the city centre, Old Durham's contrast with bustling city streets could not be greater.

Old Durham's gentle riverside slopes have been cultivated since at least Roman times. Stonework identified as part of a villa bath house and hypocaust was uncovered, but then buried again by sand and gravel quarrying near Old Durham farm in the early 1940s. Further discoveries led archaeologists to conclude that a native farmstead was established here, its Romanised occupants enjoying the kind of 'civilised' comforts usually found further south in first-century Britain.

Knowledge of this ancient community, active in the area long before the arrival of the 'Haliwerfolc' (St Cuthbert's people), may have lingered and been remembered in Old Durham's name. There is no supporting evidence but some later antiquarians even contended that Old Durham was a 'town of the Brigantes' – supposedly northern England's largest Iron Age tribe. Yet a fertile and well-drained location does make it possible that some land usage continued, and in the twelfth century Old Durham was first recorded as a manor. Like much else, it was then church land (owned by St Nicholas) and in 1268 was used for a small chapel.

From 1443 until the Dissolution, it was included in the estate of Kepier Hospital and an inventory of Old Durham's manor house in 1592 lists 'a hall and many chambers'. Accommodation was also provided for household men-at-arms in what has been described as a 'modest' medieval building.

But the suppression of the monasteries brought new masters to Old Durham. A decade after the estate was seized by the Crown in 1546, Kepier and Old Durham were purchased cheaply by John Heath, a prosperous London merchant. Durham was the place to be for the Heath dynasty however, and by the mid-seventeenth century, a Heath successor (another John) was firmly installed at Old Durham. He breathed new life into the property, beginning to lay out formal gardens to equal those at Kepier, which seasoned traveller Celia Fiennes admired greatly in 1698. Yet Old Durham's broad garden terraces, impressive central gazebo and stairways set it apart. Towards the end of the eighteenth century, although little remained of the Heaths and then the Tempests family seat, their gardens had become a thriving public attraction. Similar to the peninsula's 'hanging gardens', Old Durham was described as 'a place of sweet retirement', where summertime music was played and refreshments served.

Other popular attractions, including a pub, dances and sports, were added later, but an allegedly rowdy (or perhaps unprofitable) 'Pineapple Inn' was shut down in 1926. After the Second World War, the gardens went into what some feared would be terminal decline. Rescue came in the shape of Durham Council who purchased the site in 1985, followed by the voluntary 'Friends of Old Durham Gardens', formed in 2010.

Now well on the way to accurate restoration, Old Durham is open to the public once more. Bowling and putting greens may never be seen at Old Durham again, but its landscaped gardens might be recognised by the stylish Jacobean gentleman who first created them.

Old Durham.

Silverlink Bridge.

Regarded by journalist Frank Rushford to be 'well into the country' in the 1950s, Old Durham retains an air of rural secrecy. Yet trains once steamed through the estate before crossing the river on their way to Elvet station (finally closed in 1954). A former railway embankment now makes a useful local footpath, which leads to the unstable-looking (and feeling) Maiden Castle suspension bridge, built in 1974. An even more unusual example lies waiting nearby in Pelaw Wood. Opened in 1938, the Silverlink footbridge is said to have been inspired by the design of the rather larger Victoria Falls Bridge over the Zambezi.

4. Buried Gates and Broken Walls

Unlike York's old city walls for example, Durham's ancient defences are more secretive. Expanses of them have been ground down or withered away over the centuries, leaving comparatively little to see. Yet somehow this makes following their paths and tracing their shadowy remains all the more fascinating.

Durham's rock-studded peninsula has always stood proud as a natural defence and the Norman invaders capitalised on this with a motte-and-bailey wooden fortress, which was gradually replaced by stone after 1072. By the mid-twelfth century, the citadel of castle and cathedral was enclosed by a wall, lyrically described by the monk Laurence to be 'broad and high and strong, capped by lofty battlements with threatening towers at intervals'. Although perhaps not as powerfully built, a further circuit of wall was added at the beginning of the fourteenth century, gathering in Durham's surrounding town with the marketplace and the church of St Nicholas as its northern boundary.

Gates penetrated the walls at strategic points, the most impressive of them guarding the castle on its more vulnerable northern flank. For centuries this great North Gate towered over what is now the end of Saddler Street, and while it helped to prevent the castle ever being taken, it fell victim to the more modern demands of the humble horse and carriage. It was finally demolished in 1821. Some years before, in a final act of defiance, the gate's ancient portcullis had unexpectedly clattered down and temporarily blocked off the entire area.

A vaulted passageway led from the old North Gate into Owengate and although nothing of these romantic structures is now visible above street level, resilient chunks of the North Gate are deeply embedded in several house foundations at the head of Saddler Street and Owengate. Public access to these architectural scraps is understandably limited but close by, a two-storey bastion is often missed behind a closed street door. It was built in the early fourteenth century as part of the barbican which strengthened the North Gate. One of Durham's 'threatening towers', it now stands quietly behind a gents' hairdresser.

Not far away, some puzzling stonework halfway down Dun Cow Lane is often walked past casually. More time is usually devoted to the carved relief on the cathedral wall opposite depicting the legendary discovery of Durham as Cuthbert's final resting place. Behind you however, the rendered surface on the side of Abbey House has been cut away to expose the outline of a medieval arch and possibly a stairway. This is believed to be part of the Sid Gate or Side Gate, a further link in a chain of baileys, which in time of war could become independent compounds held by castle defenders until forced to retreat into the great keep behind them.

Further down the lane, on the falling slope from the castle hill, the church of St-Mary-Le-Bow stands at the entrance to Bow Lane. It has been a heritage centre since 1978. Before entering, look up above the doorway to notice another blind arch. It is thought to have guarded the inner bailey wall which led to King's Gate and onwards to a river ford and a wooden bridge far below. Alongside St Mary's, behind several fine houses now part of the university, are scattered more pieces of the city's time-worn walls. Their military function long since dispensed with, they have become, like the rest of old Durham's once mighty fortifications, little more than decorative curiosities.

Dun Cow Lane and Bow Lane have their own secret history. Dun Cow's name came into more general usage because of the cow and milkmaid panel, heavy-handedly restored by George Nicholson in the 1790s. The lane was formerly the site of Lydgate, a place where coffins were traditionally laid down on their last journey to the grave. A short distance away, an arch or 'bow' in the bailey wall logically gave the name to both St Mary-le-Bow and Bow Lane. And if you look closely along the pavement at the junction of the lanes, there is a kink or bow. More difficult to place are the 'Broken Walls', a site near the cathedral, high above the riverbank, where quarrying destroyed sections of city defences.

Below left: City Wall at Watergate.

Below right: St Mary-le-Bow.

'Lydgate' on Dun Cow Lane.

5. Busy Bee

On any list of Durham's best known and most accomplished writers, Jacob Bee would probably appear near the bottom. He was a contemporary of England's most celebrated diarist and while Bee's journal can never rival the depth and sophistication of Samuel Pepys, his distant voice deserves to be heard.

Bee's diary is almost 300 pages long but is unfortunately short on details of his own life. Information gleaned from other sources however tells us that he was a parishioner of St Margaret's church, Crossgate, where he was born in 1636 and buried seventy-five years later. From what has survived, this Durham scribe seems to have come to diary-keeping relatively late in life, as the events he chronicled cover the years from 1681 until a few years before his death in 1711.

Writing may have provided some solace for Bee as he tried to make a living in the leather trade while coping with private grief – all five children, born after his marriage in 1658, died before him.

After being apprenticed to Thomas Wall in Claypath, Bee became a skinner and glover by trade. A major (and smelly) local industry, leather working was first documented in the city in 1429 but must have existed beforehand. The Guild of Skinners and Glovers was established around 1507, meeting on 'Skinner's Hill' (somewhere near Elvet Bridge) and though glove making ended in the city at the end of the nineteenth century, leather manufacturing continued until the 1960s at Blagdon's riverside factory.

Jacob Bee was one of Durham's more unusual tradesmen, but his diary has neither the introspection of some other Restoration examples nor any description of his own daily working life. Instead, Bee's work is predominantly an almanac of Durham affairs, filled with entries on local births, deaths and marriages and interspersed with occasional events Bee considered worthy of inclusion.

Weather – that great British preoccupation – features strongly. Unseasonal wind and rain, a 'very fearfull thunder, with flaIshes [sic] of thunder' are recorded in May 1682, while later that year part of a cathedral window was blown in by a winter storm. Skywatching is also apparent, and Halley's Comet was described by Bee as a 'blazing stare' when it appeared over Durham in that same year.

Above all, however, Bee watched his local community. Nicknames such as 'Fatt John', 'slim Tyme', and 'Oyster Peg' are recorded with a note of warm familiarity. He also refers to Mr Ellis as 'King of the Beggars' and to the death of 'drunken' Peg Hutchinson in 1690.

Indeed, the perils of alcohol (along with falling off horses) attract several observations from the Durham diarist. Along with a drinking companion, Bee placed a bet of 'three quarts of ale' on the real age of a Mr Robert Wilson and describes in detail the inebriated state of Christopher Maskall, who 'spewed all his clothes and hatte [sic]'. Other snippets suggest that Bee, as well as drinking ale, may also have brewed and sold it. Yet whatever his business, hard times were never far away and in 1687, Bee was numbered among the 'poor' of Crossgate.

But Jacob continued to write, even when he subsequently lived as an 'outbrother' at Sherburn House, a charitable refuge for the poor (originally a leper hospital) outside the city. His original journal, thought to be lost, was rediscovered among the Surtees Raine family papers around 1913. Historians rightly see it as evidence of increasing seventeenth-century literacy rates. Yet Jacob Bee was something more. He was an ordinary man striving to be less ordinary and his diary is a faint echo of a long-lost age.

Above: Bee's Cottage on Lambton Street.

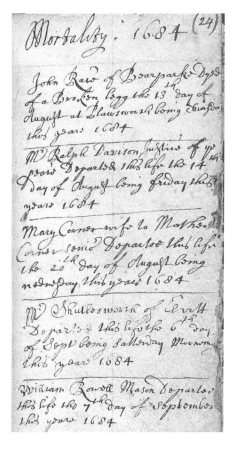

Left: Bee's diary

Although edited versions are available, reading his dog-eared and ink-stained 'booke' helps to bring Jacob Bee back to life. Collected pages from his chronicle were assembled into a narrow, leather-bound volume now held by the University Library on Palace Green. After Mr Bee was married (amusingly enough to Miss Rabbet), he is said to have lived at the entrance to Millburngate, close to Framwellgate Bridge. That district disappeared in post-war redevelopment but 'Bee's Cottage' – an old house traditionally linked to the diarist – survives further west, close to the viaduct off Sutton Street.

6. Castle in the Sky

All of Durham's ancient buildings have secret histories, but the longest must be that of the castle, parts of which are even older than the cathedral. Almost a thousand years of various uses have shaped the structure seen today.

Clues to this begin at the castle entrance on the north-west corner of Palace Green. Despite 'improvements' (or 'vandalism') by fashionable London architect James Wyatt for Bishop Barrington in 1791, characteristically bold Norman detail continues to stand out on the triple archway of the gatehouse. Wyatt's Gothicised introduction to the castle is impressive enough, but notice some suspiciously wide mortared joints on the right-hand arch. Not necessarily signs of a botched building job, they are the result of earlier alterations by Cuthbert Tunstall, Bishop of Durham between 1530 and 1559.

'Golden Old Man' Tunstall lived through turbulent times. Twice imprisoned and twice deposed during the Tudor era, he nevertheless tried to bring comfort and convenience to a castle that was losing its original purpose. Built for defence shortly after the slaughter of Durham's first Norman garrison in 1069, it required an extra dimension to be a residence fit for a prince bishop. Their high status and often lavish lifestyle was reflected in finer than usual architecture, elements of which remain but are not always easily understood. Nowhere better demonstrates this than what is now called the 'Norman Arch', the highlight of Tunstall's Gallery, which was added to the castle's north range. Dating back to the mid-twelfth-century, the crisp moulding of the upper arch must have once been sheltered by a canopy as it appears as if it was carved yesterday. Forgotten behind a plastered wall for many years, it was uncovered during the time of Barrington's restorations. Originally on an exterior wall, this Norman doorway used to be reached by a staircase from the courtyard below. Important visitors might have been ushered through the superb entrance to the bishop's apartments beyond.

The castle's public rooms have other dazzling gems. After being astonished by the scale of the Great Hall, look deeper into its baronial grandeur. Built for the imperious Anthony Bek in around 1284, it replaced an older construction, of which the undercroft still survives. In 1827, Walter Scott and the Duke of Wellington dined in the 'rude antiquity' of a hall that in fact, like much of the castle, had already undergone several facelifts. Even in troubled medieval times, Bishop Hatfield softened the Great Hall's martial appearance by creating much larger windows. More light was shed on its princely audiences and entertainments, and two fifteenth-century musicians' 'pulpits', at the south end, are later reminders of that.

More humble details, rarely commented on, are just as fascinating. Try not to be distracted too much by spectacular cross-river views from the west windows; instead look closer at their stone frames. Curious raised bosses, pierced by a central hole, protrude from some window mullions. Survivals of yet another restoration in the 1840s, they are claimed by J. R. Boyle to be copies of shutter fixings from a time when glass, even for a wealthy bishop of Durham, was a scarce luxury.

Seen from Durham's northern approach, the castle's octagonal keep, high on a mound, appears to be suspended above the city. Durham Castle evolved from stronghold to stately home and took another direction when it became an arm of the university in 1837. Nowadays it continues to accommodate students (and secrets), but has made room for 'bed and breakfast' guests as well.

Durham Castle is comparatively small, yet seems to have treasures at every turn. Among roughly 200 paintings the castle displays for instance, Bishop Tunstall's portrait is perhaps the most enigmatic. His clenched fists are not obvious signs of pent-up anger or frustration, but the result of Reformation censorship. The rosary beads he originally held were painted over. Keep a lookout also for the 'porthole' in the newel-stairway that leads from Tunstall's gallery to the courtyard below. Now cemented over, it looks suspiciously like a gun port and it points towards the Castle Gate.

Norman arch.

Above: Durham Castle.

Below: Castle keep.

7. Crossing the Water

As medieval Durham grew, new bridges became necessary to replace the peninsula's less reliable ferryboats and river fords. Built by the prince bishops, the bridges were a demonstration of their status and power and bridged the gap to Durham's boroughs and beyond. Today's visitors often use them as viewpoints for the picturesque sights around them, but may not have time to appreciate the history that lies beneath their feet.

Framwellgate, one of England's first stone bridges since Roman times, was built for the flamboyant Ranulph Flambard around 1128. Much altered over its long life, it was rebuilt after flood damage in 1401 and enlarged in the 1850s. Two broad arches now span the River Wear, but a much earlier one lies buried on the eastern bank. Bridges of this period were often lined with shops and houses, and Framwellgate had a central chapel and gatehouses guarding the castle approach. Once the threat of war diminished, the gates became a hindrance to traffic and were demolished in 1760, as the bridge gradually became a congested part of the Great North Road. Cars and buses squeezed over Framwellgate Bridge until well into the twentieth century; now, on days when it fills with pedestrians, buskers and the occasional market stall, it returns to its medieval roots.

Elvet Bridge was erected in the late twelfth century by command of Hugh Le Puiset, another ambitious bishop responsible for extensive building in Durham. Like Framwellgate, his bridge also came to have buildings along it, although Elvet had not one but two chapels facing each other across its original span, claimed to be of fourteen arches. Only ten now

Framwellgate Bridge.

Fragments of St Andrew's Chapel.

remain, one of which, on the site of St James' chapel, was used as a House of Correction from 1632 until the early nineteenth century. A section of it can still be seen and although built into a 'dry' land arch, it would no doubt have made a damp prison cell.

Prebends' Bridge, the third of Durham's trio of historic river crossings, is often regarded as the most elegant. Obviously named for its ecclesiastical pedigree, it was built by cathedral architect George Nicholson in 1772. He was advised by London-based Robert Mylne, who subsequently produced a reminiscent design for the Georgian bridge over the Tyne at Newcastle. Both men ensured that the new Durham bridge was broad enough to allow the passage of 'gentlemens' carriages' (which would also be exempt from paying a toll). Its predecessor, Dean Comber's bridge, was swept away like so many others in the catastrophic flood of 1771 – smashed remnants lie on the west riverbank upstream, a short but worthwhile stroll away, and from there the visual quality of Prebends' Bridge can be truly appreciated. It was carefully placed to complement a stunning landscape of castle, cathedral and river. Like the other ancient bridges on this stretch of the meandering Wear, time spent around and beneath them can be as enjoyable as gazing from their platforms above.

Extra ribs used to widen Framwellgate Bridge can clearly be seen when viewed from the towpath below. No trace of Framwellgate's chapel survives, but a patchwork of ancient masonry on the eastern bank of Elvet Bridge is a telltale sign. Once a blacksmith's and now a restaurant, this was St Andrew's chapel, where pilgrims could be blessed before completing their journey to St Cuthbert's shrine. Elvet Bridge was referred to as the 'new' bridge after it was built and crossing it was given a sense of occasion by locals when they said they were 'going over the water'. Large numbers are painted on its piers for the benefit of boat crews and, depending on which one they are steering through, rowing coxes call the arches 'easy arch' and 'hard arch'.

8. Durham Behind Bars

Her Majesty's Prison in Old Elvet is famous (or perhaps infamous) for the murderers and master criminals it has housed since opening in 1819. Although much altered and enlarged since then, the grim appearance of today's prison complex is only slightly relieved by its facing Assize Courts on Court Lane, an attractive Georgian design by Ignatius Bonomi who was brought in to rescue the project from early nineteenth-century 'cowboy builders'. The historic predecessors of Bonomi's gaol are now largely forgotten, but their secret remains are just as forbidding.

Records indicate an early prison building on the west of Palace Green, while the monastic community made arrangements to deal with their own offenders in the cathedral across the way. Benedictine discipline has been claimed to be not particularly harsh, but there were small prison cells near the chapter house for minor offences and a 'strong dungeon', below the Infirmary Master's lodge, to punish more serious crimes. The lodge window can be seen from the riverside path near the Galilee Chapel, and when you visit the cathedral's public toilets spare a thought for the unfortunate souls who may have once been incarcerated in chains for a year beneath your feet. They were held in what became known as the 'Lying House', though it must be pointed out that some historians are now questioning its true purpose.

Beyond doubt however, Durham's next prison was constructed early in the fifteenth century, distant from the cathedral precincts. Escapes from probably dilapidated old cells on Palace Green forced Bishop Walter Skirlaw to incorporate a new gaol into the strengthening work on the North Gate, completed by his successor Thomas Langley in 1421. For centuries this splendid building guarded the cathedral's northern approaches and was eventually embellished with all manner of heraldic shields, battlements and fanciful windows. Below them, prisoners looked forlornly out through the bars, hinting at the less than pleasant conditions inside. At the end of the sixteenth century, the prison was packed with debtors and religious dissenters, and when visited by the great prison reformer John Howard two centuries later, had showed little improvement. His description of the dungeon as the 'Great Hole' encouraged change and led to the provision of the new purpose-built establishment in Old Elvet which in 1832 came to be supervised by John Frushard, a relatively enlightened prison governor. He was also in charge of Durham's House of Correction, established in 1632 under the west end of Elvet Bridge. Prisoner transfers to the new gaol began in August 1819 and the archway buildings were sold off a few years later. Parts of them (apparently including a resident ghostly piper) have survived and are now firmly established on the tourist trail near Brown's Boathouse. But reminders of the older gaol and the North Gate – secreted below premises on Saddler Street and Owengate – are much less accessible. Beneath one shop, down a dusty stairwell and along a claustrophobic stone passageway, lies a late medieval vaulted chamber. Recent attempts seem to have been made to convert it into a storeroom. But in the gloom, rusty lengths of chain attached to the wall only add to its unnerving atmosphere.

Right: Former Gaol-Elvet Bridge.

Below: Old Newsroom.

Saddler Street basement.

On the way to the cathedral, pause at Owengate House at the junction of Saddler Street and Owengate, the site of the old North Gate and gaol. Now a hairdresser's, the shop was once a newspaper office and subscription library, one of the fee-charging establishments that began to appear in towns and cities during the eighteenth and nineteenth centuries. Fading paintwork above the doorway is just legible as 'Subscription News Rooms'. Almost as difficult to see are 'putlogs' in the façade of Old Elvet's Assize Court building. They are holes – now plastered over – made for scaffolds erected outside the prison before public executions ended in 1865.

9. Girl Power

Votes for Women may be the last thing on your mind when you enter the cathedral's north door. The famous Sanctuary Knocker generally commands most attention, while the door's rusting metal gates rarely attract a second glance. Erected during the First World War, they protected the cathedral, not from Germans but from England's female 'enemy within'.

Frustrated by the failure to achieve their ultimate goal, the women's movement became increasingly militant in the early years of the twentieth century. Protests grew from banner waving and heckling to hunger strikes and arson. Leading north-east activist Emily Davison firebombed the new house of Lloyd George in February 1913 a few months before being fatally injured at Epsom's Derby Day race meeting when she brought the king's horse down. Closer to home, there was fire-raising in Newcastle, telegraph lines were sabotaged and a railway station attacked in Durham City.

Ironically, such incidents marked the extremity of suffragette violence. Support for direct action among the various women's groups began to fall, but Durham's alarmed authorities prepared for the worst. Several cathedrals had been targeted and the bishop of Durham was determined that his would not be added to the list.

Bishop Moule received a deputation of prominent suffragettes in Durham Castle on 4 July 1914. Their discussion focused on the force-feeding of women prisoners and the 'Cat and Mouse Act' – a popular name for government legislation which released and then reimprisoned hunger strikers. The meeting appears to have been courteous and restrained (apart from the mischievous 'bangs' of paper bags outside). But when Moule promised to 'acquaint himself with the facts and communicate with the other bishops', the women probably felt he was playing cat and mouse with them.

The situation was overtaken by events much further afield. At the declaration of war in August 1914, the suffragettes officially suspended their activities. Threats rumbled on however and the following year, after a further suffragette 'scare' in Durham, the outer iron doors were installed. Partial suffrage was gained at the end of the war and women were finally awarded full voting rights in 1928, but the cathedral gates remained and are still locked every night. Showing signs of age but still solid, they are an unlikely reminder of England's all too real battle of the sexes.

Yet even if the suffragettes had forced their way through the iron grilles, they might have faced a greater spiritual barrier within. Prejudice against women was built into the cathedral and a band of Frosterley marble, crossing the west end of the nave near the font, was the closest any woman could approach the all-male preserve of St Cuthbert's shrine in medieval times.

Numerous anecdotes surround Cuthbert's supposed aversion to women. In life he was said to have asked for 'no women to come near him' and after his death, some women who tried to are claimed to have been struck down dead. But other stories tell of Cuthbert's good relations with women and of those healed by his intervention. The first person to be cured at Durham was a woman and the last documented 'miracle' at his shrine was during the visit of Princess Margaret to Durham in 1503. It has been suggested that Durham's celibate Benedictine monks invented Cuthbert the misogynist when they replaced the community of St Cuthbert – many of them married – at the end of the eleventh century. Perhaps it's just as plausible then that a tolerant saint would have sympathy with the suffragette battlecry, 'Deeds not Words'.

Cathedral North Door Gate.

Boundary Cross.

Feminists ruffled cathedral feathers long before the suffragettes. 'The Rites of Durham', which appeared originally in 1539, tells of two Newcastle serving girls 'clothed in male attire' who attempted to breach Cuthbert's sanctuary in 1417. As punishment, they were compelled to parade, still dressed as men, around their hometown churches. Such 'audacious' women of course, trying to progress in a man's world, rarely appear in the pages of history. Female members of the Porter family for instance, born on Bow Lane in the late eighteenth century before moving to Scotland, became successful writers but now receive little attention. Another author – Isobel Violet (nicknamed 'Violent') Hope, born in Old Elvet in 1862, is similarly overlooked.

10. Going Underground

Durham City still holds secrets of the time when 'coal was king'. The prized fuel was extracted around the city for centuries by way of shallow drift mines or 'bell' shaped pits. Then, in the early nineteenth century and within sight of the cathedral, coal started to be mined from deeper shafts. A vintage photograph, taken from the south-east, shows the headstock and blackened chimney of Elvet Colliery crouched less than a mile from the cathedral. After a failed attempt in the previous year, the pit began to raise coal in 1828. Described later as a 'small landsale' pit, much of its output was destined for domestic use. As a provision of the lease, reduced price coal was also made available to the local poor. This may have been still profitable for initial owners Backhouse and Mounsey who paid royalties to the Dean and Chapter, but it was disastrous for nearby St Oswald's.

The twelfth-century parish church on Church Street, probably built on an earlier religious site, was said to be on the brink of collapse after mining subsidence in 1834. 'Shaken by coal mines', the 'shut up' church of St Oswald's was extensively rebuilt by local architect Ignatius Bonomi. Two more renovations followed over the next fifty years. During the first shoring up, both the chancel and north aisle were reconstructed. A finely decorated medieval ceiling and other original features were destroyed in what has been debatably described as 'tasteless' restoration.

Much of this may not be immediately apparent to the general visitor who will enjoy this gem of a church regardless. St Oswald's has several architectural oddities which display the mismatch between 'old and new', but more obvious perhaps, and much stranger, are some of the woodcarvings peering down from the ceiling supports. Variously described as 'grotesques' or 'bearded men', they are fortunate survivors from the lost hammerbeam roof.

Coal mining's unintended consequences seem to have continued at Elvet Colliery. Further expensive damage was caused in the area before serious flooding closed the pit in 1908. Coal shafts were often named after local dignitaries, owners, their wives or family members. Around Durham City there was the Florence and Lord Ernest pit. One of Elvet's was called the 'Hazzard'. Hard labour was replaced with effort of a more intellectual kind at Elvet Colliery. The university's science campus was built on the reclaimed pithead and the 'Bill Bryson' Library, opened in 2012, now occupies the Stockton Road site. Yet the old colliery has continued to cause trouble. During the recent construction work, three historic mineshafts had to be reinforced and there is yet another nearby. Rarely noticed, the base of a ventilation chimney lies on the high riverbank. Close to St Oswald's, beneath this low ring of brickwork, are the mine workings which once threatened the church.

Other local pits worked on after Elvet closed. Collieries surrounded Durham City – Sidegate's Durham Main closed in 1924 and its neighbour at Aykley Heads (now County Hall) produced coal gas until 1949. Most important among others was Framwellgate Moor's 'Old Pit', now marked only by a terrace of distinctive white cottages which bear its name.

More fragments of mining heritage linger around the city outskirts. To the north-east in Kepier Wood – a secret treasure itself – forgotten pits and the derelict outbuildings of abandoned drift mines are concealed in tangled woodland on the riverside. On the city's opposite side, most poignant of all is the 'lost' village of Houghall. Finally demolished in 1955, only the skeletal foundations of this typical pit village can now be seen. More than industrial debris, they are rapidly disappearing monuments from an industry which cut short so many lives. They are a reminder of the true price of coal.

Industrial debris as folk art in Kepier Wood.

St Oswald's roof grotesque.

Riverbank Coal.

Durham City's coal was extracted from the colourfully named Hutton, Harvey, Busty, Brockwell and Low Main seams. They could range in thickness from a few inches to a few yards – from the commercially worthless to the profitable and prized. Outcrops of coal occur around the riverbanks but, depending on seasonal woodland growth, can be difficult to see. By Prebends' Bridge, however, some 'black diamonds' can be found. Almost invisible, there is a thin streak of coal near the foot of the quarried rock face. Reach under its sandstone ledge and get Durham's coal dust on your hands.

11. Grave Matters

Writing in 1951, Frank Rushford memorably (and with a touch of the macabre) titled Durham as the 'City of the Coffin'. He was of course referring to the arrival of the saint's body on the peninsula in 995 and the evolution of the cathedral and city around his tomb. But Durham has innumerable coffins, many of them in forgotten and lonely graveyards.

Many Durham students will have neither the time nor inclination to notice the graveyards on their own doorstep. One of them lies opposite the timber and glass frontage of the university's new Palatine Centre on Stockton Road. A green triangle of land, it might appear unused until tombstones are glimpsed between the trees.

Stockton Road cemetery was created in the final decade of the nineteenth century as an extended burial ground for St Oswald's parish church to the north. By then St Oswald's graveyard was bisected by Church Street and had expanded from a roughly circular plot, possibly pre-Conquest, around the church.

The graves in Stockton Road are now rarely visited. They are isolated from the main churchyard, which includes prominent memorials such as the Great War cross, a tall monument dedicated by Bishop Hensley Henson in 1921. Yet, since their recent formation, the Friends of Stockton Road Cemetery have worked hard to raise the profile of this neglected area.

As well as cutting back tangled weeds and planting flowers, they have peeled back decades of history, uncovering the tombstone of Mrs Mavin for example, wife of a Victorian businessman who has a nearby street named after him. In partnership with the local authority, the 'Friends' have also laid out plans to enhance and protect this restful place. More work is needed but the main gate now stands open to receive passing visitors and volunteers (including students willing to lend a hand!).

Another secret cemetery is squeezed into woodland between the railway and the road on Redhills Lane. Gravestones are dotted down the slope towards St Bede's mortuary chapel, built in 1867 for interments from the Catholic church of St Godric's in Castle Chare. Now redundant, the chapel has been converted into 'Bede Lodge', a private house. Undisturbed, the owners can enjoy its built-in curiosities – a medieval lancet widow, and (according to Pevsner), a piscina or altar bowl, both from a thirteenth-century chapel near Chester-le-Street.

St Bede's has a new lease of life but sadly, on the opposite side of the city, a similar chapel appears close to death. Locked and forlorn, the mortuary chapel of St Nicholas now lies empty at the centre of an overgrown hillside cemetery just to the north of Claypath. It was consecrated in 1861 when St Oswald's and St Mary's were unable to take any more burials from the neighbouring parish of St Nicholas. Once enclosed by high walls, the old graveyard around the medieval St Nicholas had been steadily eroded by an expanding marketplace and there were no more burials shortly after the land was sold to the City Corporation in 1841.

But while 'St Nics' chapel waits to be rescued, Claypath has another secret to reveal. A much earlier community of 'Friends' – the Quakers – built a small Meeting House there in 1675.

It was later extended and then sold off in 1873, but a few memorials from its accompanying cemetery survive, closed in by buildings and gardens behind the busy road. Even staff at the local estate agency are unaware of the tombstones not far from their desks. Quaker members have access to the Claypath graveyard to spend time in this unique spot. Its tombstones are uniformly laid flat. Dignified and unassuming, they are a reflection of the Quaker way of life.

Stockton Road Cemetery.

Above: Quaker Gravestones.

Right: St Nicholas' Chapel.

In total, St Oswald's actually has four cemeteries. Apart from the original in the church precincts, there is one on the opposite side of Church Street (opened in 1889 and now a play area), Stockton Road Cemetery and one further south on Elvet Hill Road, shared by the cathedral and university.

12. The Great, the Good and the Forgotten

On 3 May 1311, Anthony Bek was buried in Durham Cathedral with the pomp and circumstance that surrounded much of his life. So great was his prestige that he was the first bishop of Durham to be buried inside the cathedral. In a lavish ceremony officiated by the Archbishop of York, his tomb was 'covered with a cloth of deep blue and gold' and placed in the Chapel of Nine Altars, the cathedral's most sacred place. But no richness remains today and Bek, arguably the greatest prince bishop of all, now lies largely unnoticed.

Bek was a contemporary of Edward I, and although an ordained priest, could be as warlike as his master. He entered royal service in 1270 and accompanied young Prince Edward on the last major crusade to the Holy Land. After Edward came to power in 1272, Bek became indispensable to the English king, filling important posts such as King's Chancellor and Constable of the Tower of London before he was appointed bishop of Durham in 1283. He rode into battle with 'Cuthbert's Men' at Falkirk in 1298 and, escorted by his large retinue, was a glittering figure in Durham's history.

Born into Lincolnshire nobility around 1240, Anthony Bek studied in Oxford and had family ties with Durham, where one of his brothers served as a hereditary steward. A proven statesman and trusted advisor to the king, the reward for Bek was Durham, which would provide the 'ample revenues' to maintain his already considerable status.

Yet the new bishop cherished even grander dreams. His Durham episcopate was complicated by a tortuous dispute with the Archbishop of York, but in the struggle for supremacy, Bek's ambition was paramount. Proud and charismatic, he strove to create a more effective barrier against Scottish invasion, and though he ultimately failed to permanently enlarge his domain between Tyne and Tees, his reputation for greatness was confirmed and his 'Land of the Prince Bishops' was made more secure.

Despite that, few notice his grave today. A simple marble slab marks the final resting place of the 'Patriarch of Jerusalem', a rather pointless title conferred on Bek by Pope Clement V. Some visitors to the Nine Altars unknowingly walk over his tombstone to better appreciate William Van Mildert, the last in the line of Bek's successors, whose impressive effigy dominates the chapel's north end. A thoughtful-looking Van Mildert, book half open on his lap, seems to contemplate his own demise in this sculpture by Welshman John Gibson, carved in Rome.

The scholarly Van Mildert, in appearance 'slight and graceful', who was bishop from 1826, tried to deflect the wind of change blowing around England at that time. But where political reform went, religious reform was soon to follow. The Church of Durham's inflated income and the institution of prince bishop itself (though only ceremonial then) was living on borrowed time.

Above: Van Mildert.

Right: Wrench Tomb.

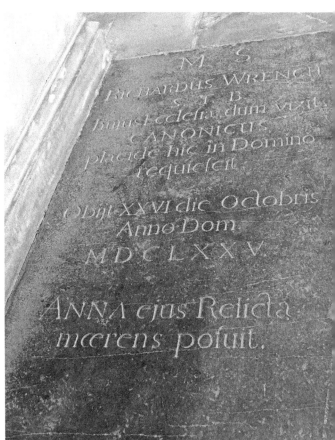

Bek's Tomb.

Van Mildert, the highest of 'High Church' men, is also remembered for his major role in founding Durham University, while Charles Thorp, his advisor, is sometimes overlooked. Despite his various ecclesiastical offices, Thorp remained true to his church at Ryton on Tyne, where he was buried in 1862. By then the long reign of Durham's Prince Bishops was over. It died with Van Mildert in 1836. Ignoring the family vault prepared for him in Auckland Castle, the religious authorities buried Van Mildert – 'Last Count Palatine of Durham' – in the cathedral. He rests under the carpet, right in front of the high altar.

Bek's tombstone is made from Frosterley 'Marble', which is not strictly a true marble but polished limestone from Weardale. His dark-stone slab is speckled with fossils and contrasts with a brass plate fixed on it in 1837. Another memorial is more obscure yet just as illuminating. Richard Wrench also lived through turbulent times. Vicar at Heighington and rector of Boldon, his Royalist sympathies forced him out of a teaching post at Cambridge until the Restoration, when he returned to Durham. Rejoicing in the title 'Prebend of the Sixth Stall', he was buried in 1675 and is found halfway down the nave near the north aisle.

13. Hidden Hall

'Hidden gem' can be an overused term, but nothing better describes Crook Hall. Over 800 years old, it is found at the fringe of the city, on a usually quiet Frankland Lane. Building on the present site began around the thirteenth century and in some ways has never stopped.

Crook Hall began as part of 'Sydgate' (now 'Sidegate'), a riverside manor acquired in the early 1300s by Peter le Croke, after whom the house was probably named. Built during dangerous times of border conflict and isolated from Durham's protective walls, the surviving Great Hall may well have needed the lancet windows and a defensive ditch, which historian Martin Roberts refers to.

One early owner would have appreciated such warlike measures. John de Coupland, English hero at Neville's Cross, is alleged to have been at Crook Hall in the hours before battle and briefly owned a half share of the manor before selling it on in 1360. More significant though were the Billingham family, owners between 1372 and 1667. Although his generosity later became a source of dispute, Thomas Billingham permitted spring water to be piped from 'Framwell Meadow' on his elevated estate, across the river into the marketplace 'pant' in 1450. (This was an obscure term for a public water trough, suggested by Henry Gradon logically enough to derive from 'panting' with thirst). Pipework terminated in the market (unless you were a Billingham family member) and though cut off temporarily by Cuthbert Billingham in 1636, the pant was the city's main supply until the mid-nineteenth century. Crook Hall's roll call of notable owners and occupiers also included seventeenth-century antiquarians and manuscript collectors Christopher and James Mickelton, the Hopper family of Shincliffe and Durham's 'indefatigable' nineteenth-century historian, James Raine.

Crook Hall evolved with them all, and extended and adapted to provide increasing domestic comfort. Doors and windows were blocked, old timbers plastered over and stairs laid on top of stairs during successive phases of development. A walk through the Great Hall today is a trip through architectural time. Below a Mickelton inscription and a date for 1671, the main doorway now leads through the ancient 'screens passage' dividing the Jacobean wing from a finely restored Great Hall. Supported by thick and roughly built walls, Le Croke's fourteenth-century hall has retained its minstrel's gallery, which was converted to bedrooms as early as the Elizabethan period. In the nineteenth century, John Fowler – obviously a practical man – used the tempting medieval space for cart storage and ale bottling. Businesslike hooks still project from heavy roof beams and Victorian beer bottles are also on display.

Yet further west from the original hall, Billingham and Mickelton's 'home improvements' were superseded by more ambitious work. A grander wing was added by the Hoppers in 1736 and their three-storey brick extension, new granary and farm buildings greatly

Crook Hall.

Mickelton Window at Crook Hall.

Crook Hook.

enlarged Crook Hall. They lived and entertained in fashionable Georgian surroundings and a plaster dove and basket (or hopper), symbolising the family name, decorates the ceiling of a genteel first-floor drawing room.

Crook Hall is also haunted. The 'White Lady' is said to be a spectral member of the Billingham family. Modern visitors can make their minds up about her but there is no doubt that Crook Hall has cast a spell on many of its owners, particularly the most recent.

From its description as 'semi-derelict' in the late 1920s, Crook Hall and gardens are unrecognisable today. Building on the efforts of their predecessors, the hard work and enthusiasm of present owners Keith and Maggie Bell has ensured the rescue of what Peter Clack has called 'a magnificent group of buildings'. Shy and retiring it may still be, but Crook Hall is coming out of its shell.

More than one visit may be needed to notice some of the hall's unusually painted ceiling beams. The Fram Well squats forgotten near the railway viaduct on Sidegate, a short walk to the south-west of Crook Hall. The sandstone well head was restored and moved there in 1959, not far from its original site.

14. In and Out

By their very nature, Durham's vennels are secret places. They are both inviting and slightly disturbing – entrances to unseen places and exits to the unexpected. An odd northern word, vennel derives from the old French 'venelle' (and in turn from the Latin for vein), meaning a narrow passageway between buildings. The term is used in Scotland, Northern Ireland and of course Durham, where numbers remain, but further south, 'ginnel' or 'gennel' is its equivalent.

Some of these ancient alleyways are well known and still used in Durham; others hardly attract a glance, half-hidden by generations of later buildings. Vennels leading off from Saddler Street for instance, are steep and sometimes slippery routes between the upper and lower town, but they are also paths which lead to medieval Durham.

As mentioned elsewhere, the Drury Lane vennel goes down through Durham's Georgian theatreland from Saddler Street to Elvet waterside. Yet Moatside Lane, almost opposite, goes much further. As self-explanatory as it seems, Moatside's name may also refer to the Norman castle mound or motte which still rises above it. Yet all agree that it follows the path of a dry moat, filled in during the seventeenth century, which, along with the Great North Gate, once defended the castle's weakest spot.

At the top of Moatside Lane, the castle keep (rebuilt from a ruin in the nineteenth century) captures most attention, while views towards the back of Saddler Street are usually ignored. This jumble of buildings however – a curiously satisfying muddle of roofs and walls – says much about the town's origins. Like other medieval settlements, Durham's grew haphazardly without any coherent plan. An impossibly cramped site only added to the pressures of construction, but it created the framework on which the town was raised and continues to be adapted.

Early tenements built end-on to Saddler Street, sometimes up to three storeys high, were entered from the narrow gaps between them. And although most were subsequently built over, some fortunately live on as the vennels of today. Centuries on, they manage to preserve something of their medieval identity. Further down Saddler Street, one of them is now home to cafés, booksellers and craft workshops. As if that wasn't enough history repeating itself, shoppers duck in and out of side openings to allow others to edge past them in the confined space.

Palace Green and the cathedral have their own vennels, with dramatic names perhaps fitting their less domestic surroundings. Both lead on to riverside paths: 'Windy Gap' (formerly Windy Nook) on the site of the lost Windishole postern and the mysterious 'Dark Entry', a shadowy tunnel from the cathedral precincts, once part of another vanished gate.

Other vennels though further away are worth finding – walk through them if you can. The Old Shire Hall's vivid brick entrance (a red rag to Pevsner's Bull) is perfectly framed by a vennel in Old Elvet and silence now reigns in Tinklers' or Tinkers' Lane in Claypath.

Yet over them all I favour the nameless ones which still hang on around old Walkergate. This often forgotten riverside district, below the back of Silver Street, was congested with industry and warehousing as it fell into decline. Few signs of that remain, but some of its passageways continue to spill down the slope. Barred by heavy gates, they are now stairways to nowhere, neglected and unkempt. Nevertheless, like all the others, they are important connections with Durham's past.

Dark Entry.
Inset: Drury Lane Vennel.

Medieval vennels were open or covered, but their maintenance was deemed to be a public responsibility. It's also possible they could act as primitive fire barriers between highly combustible early structures. Walking down one today, however, it seems likely that flames would quickly bridge such narrow gaps. Yet it appears that although largely deprived of their original purpose, some vennels now serve as galleries for the budding graffiti artist.

15. Let There be Light (and Indoor Plumbing)

Early nineteenth-century Durham was a dark and insanitary place. The city was said to be 'notorious for its nocturnal darkness' and unpaved streets were used as dung heaps and slaughterhouses. Butchers were once busy on the roadway in Saddler Street, in a quarter known as 'Fleshergate'. However, prospects brightened when the Durham Paving Commissioners (a body also charged with street cleaning, lighting and other public services) employed local contractors to install oil lamps across the town. In 1821 roughly 180 lamps, burning 'best Greenland whale oil', glowed in the city. The new lights seemed to be as popular for smashing and stealing as they were for providing illumination. But then as now, new technology was appearing and gaslight, claiming to be four times brighter and costing the same as oil, was soon adopted. By 1824, Durham's gas company was piping coal gas around the city from their gasworks by the river at Framwellgate, lighting gas lamps with the flickering, greenish flame familiar on Durham streets until well into the twentieth century. Incandescent gaslight was superseded by electricity and modern reproductions of gas lamps now add to Durham's period charm. Few originals have survived the scrapyard, but some have been converted and shine on around Palace Green and the cathedral precincts.

Placed more conspicuously in the bailey, yet generally ignored, is a much stranger contraption. On the roadside, beneath rust and peeling paint, is the base and column of a sewer gas lamp. These odd devices were the work of Birmingham builder-cum-inventor Joseph Webb and were installed worldwide after 1900.

Cholera had a devastating impact on Britain during the nineteenth century. Sanitation measures were belatedly introduced to stop the spread of disease; following the Public Health Act of 1848, water quality and sewerage slowly improved. Durham's Board of Health built new sewers to replace the foulest 'open gutters and ditches' and insisted on the proper connection of household drains to the sewer system. Toxic and lethal gases could accumulate underground, however, and explosions were not unknown. Joseph Webb's Gas Destructor was one response to this. Patented in the 1890s, it was powered mainly by town gas but was also linked to the local sewer, ventilating and burning off noxious fumes. With typical Victorian flair, Webb helped to light the world above from the darkness below.

Webb's devices were fitted at high points in the sewer network, so a sad relic at the top of Redhills Lane outside St Bede's cemetery might initially be thought to have been manufactured in one of his Birmingham or London factories. Today, only a battered stump remains of what is almost certainly instead one of Durham's last 'stink pipes' – tall and hollow tubes which were simple venting devices fitted widely after the infamous 'Great Stink' from London's sewers in 1858. Peel back some ivy from a heavily corroded pole in nearby Ainsley Street, on a forgotten path below the Miners' Hall, and see for yourself. A similar pipe, just as rusty, stands at the foot of Redhills Lane and another, as tall as a tree, is in a car parking area at Pimlico, just off Quarryheads Lane.

Durham's electricity supply caused another kind of stink. Electricity began to be supplied to the city at the beginning of the twentieth century and plans were afterwards laid for a massive power station at Kepier. Fortunately, County Durham-born town planner Thomas Sharp spearheaded rejection of the 1944 scheme. Cooling tower smoke, drifting over the peninsula, would have been a spectacle definitely not worth seeing.

The Elvets were among Durham's first districts to be lit by oil lamps. Two centuries later, one lamp bracket can still be seen. Search for it on railings outside the elegant town houses near the prison at the end of Old Elvet's 'fine wide street'. More contemporary lighting raises fewer eyebrows. Most customers entering Claypath's Tandoori restaurant are oblivious to an unusual lamp above their heads. Shaped as a flaming torch, it once shed light on a police station and then a library which occupied the site.

South Bailey Sewer Lamp.

Above: Webb Nameplate.

Below: Old Elvet Lamp Holder.

16. Little, Large and Tall

A 'Polish Dwarf', a larger-than-life thespian and a Cathedral Worthy, may sound like fictional characters from a modern farce, but they were real-life contemporaries who all lived and died in nineteenth-century Durham.

Little Count Joseph Boruwlaski is best known among them. His memoirs, published in three editions between 1788 and 1820, are now rarely read. Yet behind their fussy prose is the story of a man who was small in stature but strong in personality. His journey to the City of Durham took half of his long life. He retired there in 1791 to what he called 'his quiet place'. Before then, he had travelled widely across Europe, serenading the crowds with his musical talents wherever he could, but always dependent on patronage and regular financial gifts from the gentry.

From an early age he was determined that his lack of inches would not hold him back. Only 8 inches tall at birth, he remarkably survived and though he only reached 39 inches as an adult, he resolved to 'arm myself with patience and prudence against the evils and changes of life'. But the education he received from the Polish aristocrats who adopted him, and lessons in music and dance, were key to his success. Subsequent journeys across remote and sometimes dangerous parts of eastern Europe were tackled with the courage of a man twice his size. It broadened his knowledge and helped him to become more than the 'jou-jou' or 'plaything', which some female admirers called him. (In later years, an ample lady – described as his 'valet' – carried him through the streets of Durham.) Witty and well informed, Boruwlaski's lively conversations impressed his many acquaintances and friends. Close among these was Stephen Kemble (another great raconteur), who, similar to the Little Count, was a star of Durham's social scene in the early nineteenth century. Kemble, who also chose 'quiet' Durham for retirement, was a leading light in Britain's world of entertainment.

Born in Kington, Herefordshire, in 1758 into a renowned theatrical clan, he trained briefly as a surgeon before following in his father's footsteps. Young Kemble went on to establish a lasting north-east connection and in 1791 became manager of Newcastle's original Theatre Royal on Moseley Street. Many other halls, large and small followed, and by 1815 Kemble directed and acted in theatres across Britain (including Durham.) Yet though he was playwright and poet as well, Kemble found fame mainly for his acting skill. Shakespearean parts were his forte, and his portrayal of Falstaff in particular was roundly praised. But as Kemble's fame increased, so did his weight. Various estimates are given of it in later life (between 18 and even 30 stones) but even though it limited his acting career, his bulk seems to have added even greater realism to his best and most popular comic role.

Kemble attracts smaller audiences now. His portrait, copied from Sir Thomas Lawrence by local artist Clement Burlison, is in Durham Town Hall. High on the wall, and difficult to see in the subdued light, it captures a sleek-looking Kemble in costume as Hamlet. A painting of Kemble's diminutive friend hangs nearby and some accounts claim the two characters were buried beside each other as well. But in September 1837, fifteen years after Stephen Kemble was laid to rest in the Chapel of the Nine Altars, Boruwlaski was buried near the North Door, at the cathedral's opposite end. Next to him in fact, also beneath a simple floor slab, lies John Leybourne, who died in 1822. Referred to in White's burial records as the count's 'last earthly neighbour', he served for many years as Deputy Treasurer and Receiver to the Dean and Chapter. Obituaries say Leybourne (like Boruwlaski) was 'generally esteemed a kind and warm-hearted friend'. Unlike the Little Count, however, his final companion was a rather tall man.

Below left: The Little Count.

Below right: Boruwlaski Monument.

Entrance to St Mary-the-Less.

There is a tribute to Joseph Boruwlaski, appropriately enough, in the little church of St Mary-the-Less. Everything is small about this building in the South Bailey. Originally built to serve the castle garrison, it had a tiny 4-acre parish and is 'Less' because it shelters behind the 'Great' church of St Mary, otherwise known as Durham Cathedral. In a building at the gate of St Mary-the-Less can be seen fragments from its medieval rectory. A fine Gothic memorial dedicated to the Little Count by architect J. A. Cory is inside the church – enthusiastic rector James Raine placed it there after it was rejected by cathedral officials. Kemble inspired no similar tributes, but 'The Grove', the large house at the top of South Street where he spent his final decade, remains. He may also have been pleased that a distinctive half-timbered building at No. 62 Saddler Street, now an art shop and gallery, is named after him. Next door is the Shakespeare Tavern, on the site of one of the local theatres which Kemble knew well. (His final curtain call was in Durham a few weeks before his death.) The theatre was burned down in 1869, but a solitary gable wall from it survives at the back of the pub.

17. Men of Many Parts

For such a tall structure, Durham's railway viaduct has maintained a low public profile. It has never won an architectural award and features in few guidebooks, but goes about its daily job of carrying Durham's main north–south rail line in a quietly efficient way. Comprising eleven arches, the viaduct soars 100 feet in the air and looks out over the city from the head of North Road. Views unfold from the station on top that are known the world over but the viaduct itself has somehow faded into the background, rather like the men who created it.

Even though a local station opened at Gilesgate in 1844, national rail services were late to arrive in Durham City. Some delay was caused by 'difficulties' (according to 'Railway King' George Hudson), from the landowning Dean and Chapter and it was not until 1872 that direct travel to London or Scotland was possible from the North Road platforms.

Afterwards, the city viaduct became a vital artery on the East Coast Main Line, but its construction began in 1853 only as part of a branch line to Bishop Auckland. The route proposed by the North Eastern Railway was over some tough terrain – requiring two more substantial viaducts – but the railway company's newly appointed chief engineer was well equipped to meet the challenge.

Thomas Elliot Harrison was born in London in 1808, but came north with his family when he was a child. After education at Kepier Grammar in Houghton-le-Spring, and an apprenticeship with William Chapman's civil engineering practice in Newcastle, Harrison emerged as Britain's railway age was gathering pace.

Harrison's first employer, Robert Stephenson, not much older than his pupil, was already a driving force in railway development. He was an important influence on Thomas and also a friend, but Harrison arrived in Durham very much his own man after five years as chief of the York, Newcastle and Berwick Railway.

Unlike the other two viaducts on the line at Newton Cap and Belmont, the Wear did not need to be spanned at Durham. But the deep Flass Valley and its streams draining down toward North Road proved to be daunting. Building contractor Richard Cail was forced to use heavy oak piles, driven over 50 feet down, to support massive rectangular piers. Success achieved, building progressed and the viaduct designed by Harrison took centre stage on the new branch line which opened in 1856.

Gateshead-born entrepreneur Richard Cail, born in 1812, managed factories, owned quarries and brickworks and, after retiring from railway construction in 1859, went on to become mayor of Newcastle. He has been called a 'man of many parts', but most of them are now forgotten. Similarly, 'Honest Tom' Harrison continued to work conscientiously until the day before he died at his Whitburn home in 1888. Throughout a solid, if not spectacular, career, his services in railway, dock and bridge engineering were always in demand. Described by his biographer as 'much neglected' by historians, Harrison was certainly a great engineer, but he lived in an age of great engineers and his name has been eclipsed by legendary railway pioneers George and Robert Stephenson.

Nevertheless, Harrison and Cail have left their own monument in Durham and it curves gently into the railway station. Reinforcements have been made to the foundations and decking but overall the graceful viaduct has coped well with the demands of modern rail transport. Structural weakness is continually guarded against however, and keen eyes will detect the small stress or fracture warning plates fixed at strategic points on the viaduct's stonework.

Several fatalities occurred during the viaduct's construction. Most unusual was that of a bystander – a butcher struck by falling timber. Most poignant is the sad tale of Lancelot Shafto, who committed suicide after his cottage was knocked down to make way for the viaduct. Ironically, new terraced houses and businesses soon huddled around its wide arches. Music and metal are the secret themes here. Look up for the restored hoist on Harrison's (no relation to 'T. E') former organ works in Hawthorn Terrace. Look down for cast-iron drain covers from Hauxwell's demolished foundry in the surrounding streets.

Above left: Harrison Crane.

Above right: 'Tell-Tale'.

Right: Viaduct.

18. Moonfleet Man

'Windy Gap' seems better known for its quirky name than its most remarkable inhabitant. This narrow lane, branching off sharply from Palace Green, diverts few of the visitors who are aiming for the nearby cathedral entrance.

Place names evolve through time, and Windy Gap is no exception. Once leading to a small gate or 'postern' in the castle's bailey wall, it was originally 'Wyndshole Yett', before 'Windishole Gate', 'Windy Nook' and now 'Windy Gap' (which, on wintry Durham afternoons, it often is).

Perhaps this is one of the reasons why the plaque at a doorway of Divinity House, halfway down the lane, is so often missed. It informs us that this was the home of John Meade Falkner and goes on to describe him as 'bibliophile and author'. But this can only hint at the achievements of a man, always inspired by his surroundings, whose many talents flourished when he lived in what he referred to as his 'most delightful old house' in Durham.

Falkner's journey to Divinity House began in Manningford Bruce, a picturesque Wiltshire village, where he was born a clergyman's son in 1858. Love of classics and languages was obviously inherited from his parents, who taught him Latin and Greek, and Falkner's passion for history began to blossom during his teenage years. He cycled around his home county while at boarding school, visiting ruins and churches, and his first poetry was composed about this time. And though his subsequent university degree was mediocre, it introduced him to John Noble and the Newcastle family who shaped the rest of his life.

After graduating from Oxford in 1882, Falkner became a tutor to the son of Andrew Noble. At that time, this soldier, scientist and ballistics specialist, was effectively in charge of Sir William Armstrong's vast engineering works at Elswick on the banks of the Tyne.

Falkner became indispensable to his employer and within a few years was propelled from the relative tranquility of the Noble household in Jesmond to Tyneside's noisy industrial world. From becoming Noble's personal secretary, Falkner rose through company ranks and by 1901 was a director of newly formed Armstrong Whitworth, a worldwide supplier of ships and armaments. Falkner was important to the new company's success and his linguistic and negotiating skills proved decisive in winning foreign orders. An unlikely transition from teacher to high-flying businessman seemed complete.

Yet this hectic period was also one of the most productive for the 'other' Falkner. During the final decade of the nineteenth century, he somehow found the time and energy to publish topographical books on Oxfordshire as well as several novels, of which *Moonfleet* remains the best known. Still in print, this rousing tale was set among his childhood haunts and has been compared favourably with the best of Robert Louis Stevenson's adventure stories.

Durham was a convenient base for Falkner as well as a welcome refuge from the pressures of his demanding job. But its rich history was also a major attraction and

Back of Divinity House.

HOME OF
JOHN MEADE FALKNER
(1858 - 1932)
BIBLIOPHILE AND AUTHOR.

1923 1973

Falkner plaque.

IN MEMORIAM
JOHANNIS MEADE FALKNER A M
COLLEGII HERTFORDENSIS
IN OXONIA SOCII HONORARII
CAPITALI DUNELMENSIS
BIBLIOTHECARII HONORARII
ARTIS PALAEOGRAPHICAE
IN UNIVERSITATE DUNELMENSI
LECTORIS
NAT MDCCCLVIII OB MCMXXXII
VIRI SI QUIS ALIUS HUMANI
AMABILIS ERUDITI
QUI SCRIBENDI GRATIA
SERMONIS LEPORE
DOCTRINAE VARIETATE
CORDA OMNIUM SIBI DEVINXIT
HAVE PIA ANIMA

Falkner Memorial
in the cathedral.

he believed the cathedral to be 'the most impressive church in the world'. He lodged first in South Street, before purchasing Divinity House, headmaster's residence in the old Grammar School, in 1899. Although Falkner's health began to fail during the 1920s, his scholarly pursuits continued. He wrote church music and spent some of his considerable fortune on rare books and manuscripts. Falkner died at his beloved Divinity House in 1932 and while his tomb is in Oxfordshire, his spirit may sometimes blow through Windy Gap.

Alterations that Falkner made to Divinity House are still evident. Look at the rear of the property for bay windows, added to give their inquisitive owner superb river views. As he was gazing through the glass, he may have mused about *The Nebuly Coat*, his last published novel. It has a grand English minster, reminiscent of the cathedral on his doorstep, as its melodramatic centrepiece. Falkner's enthusiasm for Durham Cathedral could verge on the supernatural. He believed that medieval incense seeping from the venerable stonework caused the nave's occasionally hazy atmosphere.

19. Mr Henderson's Hall

Victorian town halls are rarely shy and retiring. Bold and brash, they are proud expressions of nineteenth-century civic pride and usually dominate their town centres. Durham's Town Hall is rather different, pushed into the corner of the marketplace and described as 'nicely humble' in a famous architectural guidebook. Visitors may need to be directed towards the Town Hall, but there are secret treasures behind its Tudor-esque façade.

Permission to enter the Town Hall's suite of rooms is always required. Historic as it may be, the Grade II-listed building is not a museum piece and is still used regularly. A functional reception area quickly gives way to a world of dark-wood Victoriana known as the 'Crush Hall'. More corridor than hall, but not usually as congested as it sounds, the 'Crush' is lined with memorabilia of the Polish count and racks containing Boer War weapons. Other public buildings have entrance lobbies called by this name, but in Durham's case it would be worth pushing through a crowd to enter the surprising Main Hall that lies beyond it.

If the Town Hall's exterior is muted, its Main Hall makes more noise. Not as exuberant as some of his contemporary practitioners of Victorian Gothic style, architect Philip Charles Hardwick nevertheless created something of a medieval fantasy when he designed the hall. Crowned by an elaborate hammerbeam roof, said to be a smaller version of the genuinely ancient example in London's Westminster Hall, Hardwick's spacious meeting and function room is scattered with allusions to Durham's history.

Much of the wall space is covered with armorials of prominent county families, insignias of Durham's ancient guilds and oil paintings of local politicians and celebrities (including, strangely enough, Sir Robert Peel, who died in 1850, and the poet Robert Burns, who had many local 'admirers'). High above your head are a dozen angels bearing shields – splashes of colour against the dark timber ceiling – and in the roof around them are ranged a further sixteen shields, carrying the arms of Durham's other incorporated companies.

But above all, the Main Hall's great west window looks into Durham's past and anticipates its future. In a glow of stained glass, the people of Durham step out from the surrounding nobility and churchmen. In one historical episode portrayed in the window's lower lights, a boyish Edward III rewards Durham citizens for protecting his supply wagons during the Weardale campaign of 1327. Above that, foreshadowing modern ceremonies, Durham tradesmen gather on Palace Green, their guild banners flying alongside the flag of St Cuthbert.

When the hall was opened in January 1851, one man more than any other would have appreciated it. William Henderson, mayor of Durham during 1848 and 1849, was instrumental in the Town Hall project. He was well aware that an increasingly busy and assertive Town Council had outgrown its old Guild Hall base, which started life in the mid-fourteenth century. Not only did he propose that a new and larger Town Hall should be built on to the existing civic buildings, but he was a vigorous fundraiser and made a substantial personal contribution to the public subscription.

Henderson's term of office was brief but his legacy is stamped firmly on the Town Hall. A portrait of the studious looking Henderson hangs in the Main Hall and almost an entire visit can be devoted to searching for more references to him. His name or initials appear in various parts of the building. Most difficult to find, but most fitting of all are those entwined on a large iron key. It opens 'Mr Henderson's Main Hall'.

In one colourful west-window scene in the Town Hall, the red roof glimpsed above King Edward is said by one guidebook to be the Market Place 'pant' or well, actually built in 1450, over a century after the depicted event. Less artistic licence is on show with the depiction of St Nicholas' church, however. To the left of the Royal Standard, stained-glass artist James Nixon of London has correctly illustrated the church tower as it was before 1857. Similarly, in the window light above, the west end of Durham Cathedral is accurately portrayed with two lead sheathed spires or 'broaches', which were taken down in 1658.

Opposite: Hall Stained Glass.

Town Hall.
Inset: Town Hall Keys.

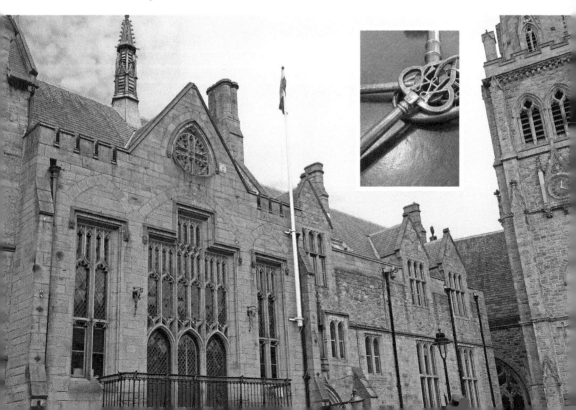

20. Music Men

Music in the cathedral enriches the Durham experience even more. For such a huge building, the cathedral has remarkable acoustics. The moving sound of choral voices or the thundering organ soars to the high roof vault and rolls across the 205-foot nave. The building's main organ is particularly fascinating. Richly decorated pipework conceals a big and complex machine linked on both north and south aisles of the choir. Set up in the 1870s and much modified since, it is the latest in a celebrated line. But rather like the modern organist, hidden from public view, the history of these fine instruments and the musicians who played them can sometimes be hard to see.

Organs have graced the cathedral for over 700 years. Any that survived the Reformation were smashed up during the Scottish occupation of Durham in 1640 or believed to have been used as firewood by Scots prisoners held in the cathedral a decade later. A new Stuart king brought stability to the borders, however, and a new organ was playing in Durham by 1662. Built by George Dallam, one of a dynasty of organ builders, it was afterwards replaced by the work of Bernard 'Father' Smith – a master of the organ makers' craft.

Born Bernhardt Schmidt in Germany, he exploited England's shortage of skilled organ builders and repairers in the late seventeenth century. After the Restoration, Smith came to dominate the trade and although the finish of his instruments was sometimes criticised, it was agreed that they sounded 'like an angel'. They are still found in this country's most prestigious locations and, not surprisingly, an example by Father Smith was erected in Durham, a few years after he became king's organ maker in 1681.

The son of a Durham shoemaker came to know this organ well. Thomas Ebdon was born near the cathedral and was baptised at St Oswald's in 1738. His ability obviously impressed and in 1763, after some time as a chorister, lay clerk and assistant, he was appointed cathedral organist at a salary of £80 a year. Not everyone in Durham's Dean and Chapter welcomed his promotion, but Ebdon was certainly a departure from his predecessor James Heseltine. Recruited from London, the imperious-looking Heseltine seems to have been as notable for his tantrums as his talent.

Nevertheless, the young and more even-tempered Ebdon grew into the job and remained in post until his death in 1811. He contributed much to Durham's significant music scene, both inside and out of the cathedral. He promoted and played at high-class concerts in the region's important towns and in 1770, with money from the sale of his Bow Lane property, turned the North Bailey Assembly Rooms into 'Mr Ebdon's Music Room'.

Ebdon was a prolific composer as well as an accomplished performer and teacher. He was also kind and compassionate – the Ebdon family were Joseph Boruwlaski's main benefactor during his final years in Durham. Perhaps Thomas Ebdon the organ-master was only a minor character in Durham's storybook, but he was the stereotypical 'local boy makes good' as well. And he made his mark in other ways. Walk past the organ along the cathedral's north aisle to look closely at the choir's outer doorframe. Ebdon's name is carved into the woodwork. It is not roughly scratched in, but fashioned by the hand of a craftsman and musician.

Father Smith's great organ had a high profile until 1846 when it was moved from a central position in the choir to the north aisle. Unrepairable by 1873, it was replaced by the Willis of London instrument now played by male and female organists. A large section of Smith's dark-oak organ case survives, however. It stands against the cathedral's south wall near the Galilee chapel and is remarkably still in use – as a cloakroom by cathedral staff!

Smith Organ.
Inset: Cathedral Choir Doorframe.

21. Name Game

Like many others, Durham's place names can be illuminating. They are a first point of entry into a secret past. But they must also be treated with caution; they are not always what they seem.

Several of them end in 'gate'. Crossgate, Framwellgate and Millburngate for instance, all once began and ended at the gated towers on Framwellgate Bridge, but owe their meaning instead to '*gata*' – the Old Norse term for road or street.

Crossgate is interesting not only because it may also allude to the city's Old Borough markers, but also because of its strategic location. The junction of Crossgate with North Road, South Street and Millburngate at Framwellgate Bridge was once popularly regarded as 'Five Ways', an ancient meeting of routes on the city's west side.

Owengate has other complications. Previously known as Queen Street, this short and steep entrance to Palace Green has reverted to its original name only within the last century. Unambiguously recorded in the fourteenth century as a 'gate called Owengate', it was surmised by Gradon to be a small inner gate within the castle defences. He also believed it was named after a long-forgotten 'Owen', but modern opinion views it instead as a corruption of 'oven', from a nearby and doubtless much frequented manorial bakehouse. But Gradon was nearer the mark with Framwellgate. It could simply mean the street that Crook Hall's well or 'strong spring' leads to or comes 'fram'– an Anglo-Saxon preposition that local dialect had no need to change.

Millburngate seems obvious enough. The Mill Burn, now buried and forgotten, once cut through a valley filled today by North Road. For centuries the burn powered two corn mills. One stood on the site of today's North Road bus station and the other was the riverside 'Clock Mill', originally owned by the priory, which operated into the nineteenth century. Most perplexing of all however is Allergate. Branching off from Crossgate, this unassuming and relatively short street is as historic as its neighbours. In Chaucer's England, 'allgates' meant all ways, but Allergate's name has even more twists and turns. A French connection (from '*allez*' meaning to go) is another contender but 'Alvertongate or Allertongate', the street's former title, is a more serious candidate. Allertonshire, the district around Yorkshire's Northallerton, regained some importance after it came under the jurisdiction of Durham's prince bishops in the late eleventh century. It will never be known if any of them passed through Allergate on the way to their Northallerton palace.

More familiar street names can also mislead. Saddler and Silver Streets, at the peninsula's hub, have their own puzzles to solve. Saddler was earlier spelt Sadler and possibly signified this once common leather trade. Butchers or 'Flesh Hewers' as well as cobblers worked in the area, so there certainly must have been no shortage of raw material. But further complications arise in the person of king's commissioner Sir Ralph Sadler, reputed to be a sixteenth-century resident. And suggestions that Silver Street had a mint or was a silver-working centre are also confusing. The bishop did have his mint, but it was securely placed within sight of his castle on Palace Green and it would take many silversmiths to christen an entire street. For Gibby and Colgrave, all this is 'a mystery' and one of the 'pitfalls which abound in the study of place names' – a fascinating mystery nevertheless. We await a Mr Silver to emerge from the history of Silver Street.

Allergate.

Tenter Terrace.

Street names can throw light on obsolete trades. Both Walkergate and Tenter Terrace recall Durham's historic wool industry. Chartered in 1565 but active much earlier, cloth workers or 'walkers' were mainstays of medieval textile production. To strengthen and clean fabric, it was laboriously tramped over by workers who bestowed their name on the Walkergate district – now a short riverside lane behind the Market Hall. Before mechanisation, the services of a 'Tenterer' were also required. In open and airy places like Tenter Terrace, above North Road, they stretched sheets of cloth to dry on frames, securing it with 'tenterhooks'.

22. Open and Shut

Where would we be without doors? Welcomed entrances and exits as well as necessary barriers between us and the outside world, they are also mundane and usually ignored pieces of domestic architecture.

Yet visitors often stand and stare outside the cathedral's North Door. Understandably, few seem to notice the ancient timber doors themselves however, as they take photographs or 'selfies' which invariably capture the famed medieval 'Sanctuary Knocker' hanging behind them.

Substituted by a far less valuable replica in 1980 (which subsequently failed to deter an attempted theft), this amazing artefact, as Dr Douglas Pocock has taken pains to point out, lacks a proper striking plate and therefore is technically not a 'knocker' at all. Nevertheless, until 1637, when the right of sanctuary was abolished, fugitives would have been relieved to grab its metal ring and briefly escape the hue and cry.

They too would have cared little about the composition of the doors. Made of exceptionally long heartwood planks (split from a single huge oak, felled between about 1109 and 1144), they are a type of mortise and tenon construction, wedged together to create a sturdy construction without the use of nails. To disguise and decorate the joints, mouldings were fixed to sections of the door faces and beneath modern wax coatings, traces of previous paint finishes have been detected.

A conservation report of the 1990s also suggests that the doors were repaired during the seventeenth century, following a period of general vandalism and neglect. Bishop John Cosin probably came to their rescue during his 'enthusiastic' restoration schemes, carried out not only in the Cathedral and Castle, but also across his diocese. But perhaps just as interesting, and (lamentably) something I have only recently noticed, is a small opening cut into the door's east wing. Made for convenience when the main entrance was shut, this smaller wicket door is called the suitably scriptural 'eye of the needle'.

And if one historic door within a door was not enough, another faces it across Palace Green, as the castle has its own version. An iron-strapped doorway, complete with wicket gate, is attributed to Bishop Tunstall's episcopate installed during his sixteenth-century enlargement of the Norman gatehouse.

Unlike their cathedral cousins, however, fewer great dramas appear to have unfolded in front of the castle doors. Less glamorously, they were the setting for an obscure ecclesiastical argument that Boyle's 1892 *Guide to Durham* assures us is 'an amusing tale'.

Nathaniel (Lord) Crewe was certainly charitable, but also appears to have been one of Durham's more manipulative bishops. His eye always on the main chance, he was described by a respected contemporary as 'a cunning man'. In 1688, during a lively argument with senior churchmen as they approached the castle gates, Lord Crewe sided with the Catholic James II rather than his own Protestant clergy. Seemingly light-hearted insults were exchanged before the prebendary of Durham, Dr Robert Grey, told the bishop that he and his likeminded friends would rather leave the castle through the open wicket gate. For men of conscience like Grey, this was the 'strait' and by implication, honest way.

Above left: Castle wicket gate.

Above centre: Sanctuary Knocker (in Brick) outside Durham Rugby Club.

Above right: Sanctuary Knocker.

Despite its great size, the cathedral's original west portal has been steadily forgotten. It was first obstructed by the Galilee chapel in the 1170s and then blocked up behind Bishop Langley's grandiose tomb in the early fifteenth century. The door was restored in 1846 and until recently served as backdrop to a reception desk. The south door to the cloisters, with its swirling medieval metalwork, has also made concessions to visitor requirements. Known as the 'monks door', much of it now shelters under a modern draught-free porch.

23. Pointing the Way

We all need pointers to direct us around occasionally. Durham City has human pointers. Enthusiastic and knowledgeable, these pink-clad guides are 'here to help' visitors. But some pointers are harder to follow. Among the cathedral's countless points of interest for instance, it's no surprise that small details can escape your attention. On the wall and pavement of the cloister's north-facing wall, for example, are some intriguingly incised 'meridian' marks. They can be difficult to spot against the honey-coloured stone.

A vertical line on the arcade wall is dated 1829, when restoration of the cloister roof had just been completed. Arrowheads on the wall and floor are labelled '*meri dies*' – Latin for midday – and opposite, like a tiny unblinking eye, is an aperture in the Cloister's unglazed window frame. Weather permitting, of course, sunshine through this pinhole (technically a 'gnomon') casts a spot of light that tracks over the meridians and can indicate the difference between Greenwich Mean and local time at noon, as well as pointing to true north.

This type of sundial, more properly termed a 'noon dial', is rare in Britain. First introduced here in around 1720, they originated in Europe's grand Catholic cathedrals. As much works of art as scientific instruments, they were used to calculate the date of Easter – a crucial time in the religious calendar.

Durham Cathedral's less ostentatious meridian was installed by Mr Carr, headmaster of Durham School in collaboration with William Lloyd Wharton of Dryburn House, just outside the city centre. Born into one of Durham's most prestigious families, lawyer and entrepreneur Wharton went on to become High Sheriff of Durham in the 1830s. He was actively involved in the development of Victorian Durham, particularly the expansion of the North East Railway and the building of a new train station on part of his Dryburn estate. And though he is well known for donating parkland later named in his honour, Wharton's finest memorial, a second and much grander meridian, is now largely forgotten.

Shrouded by trees and surrounded by railings, a slim column rises almost 100 feet above the private grounds of St Leonard's School (named after a leper hospital once nearby.) The sandstone obelisk on Western Hill was another gift from the philanthropic Wharton, this one pointing to his abiding love of astronomy and support for science at the newly founded University of Durham. Today, Wharton's needle-like structure struggles to be even a landmark. Described recently as 'a fabulous folly', it was erected in 1850 for entirely practical reasons, acting as a reliable meridian for the university's observatory. Built ten years earlier, and sitting on its own hill nearly 1 mile south, this charming little building was another local design by Anthony Salvin. Stargazing now over, the site still functions as a weather station and the building is used to store musical instruments. During the

63

nineteenth century, however, Wharton's elegant obelisk helped the observatory to carry
out significant astronomy.

Yet while this Wharton meridian is also now obsolete, the park named after him
continues to point the way forward. 'The Way' – a public art installation by Hamish
Horsley – is a new kind of meridian, in cubist-shaped forms of Portland stone. Originally
commissioned by British Rail, and first exhibited at Gateshead, the work was modified
for its relocation to the hilltop of Wharton Park in 1994. Erected to celebrate St Cuthbert
and the millennium of Durham's foundation, the Way's central avenue points not true
north, but to the cathedral's main tower.

If it were possible to clamber up the obelisk's central staircase, you would be
rewarded with bird's-eye views over Durham. Standing out towards the south-west
on Elvet Hill is St Mary's College, built in 1952 in neoclassical style. Ask to see its
sundial, a 'vertical declining' example with a bronze frame. It was installed in 1999
in memory of a former staff member.

Above left: St Mary's Sundial.

Above right: Obelisk.

24. Prison Without Cells

As if one grim Victorian prison in Durham city was not enough, it also had a penitentiary. The American-sounding County Penitentiary, however, was not built to incarcerate criminals, but to rehabilitate Durham's 'fallen women'. This term, slightly amusing to modern ears, was common currency at that time. Women were placed on a lofty moral pedestal and often became outcasts if men judged them to have fallen from it. This was particularly the case with the poor, where women, often helpless victims of poverty and abuse, were forced deeper into the dark seams of Victorian society.

Britain's first female penitentiary opened in London in 1806 but it was not until April 1852 that one of these 'Houses of Mercy', as they were also known, was established at Lower Gilesgate in Durham. Like the others, it was a charitable institution and it published rules and regulations that provide a fascinating insight into its guiding principles and daily operation. Clear intentions were set out from the start:

> The object of the Institution is to afford an asylum to females, who having deviated from the path of virtue, are desirous of being restored, by religious instructions and the formation of moral habits, to a reputable condition in society.

The driving force behind this rulebook was George Hans Hamilton, a name as dimly remembered now as the institution he championed. Irish-born Hamilton was a curate in Sunderland before his appointment as Durham prison chaplain in 1848, aged only twenty-five. According to historian Ruth Cranfield, this was a 'great time of prison chaplains' and Hamilton was one of the most notable. Tackling his new role with vigorous efficiency, he quickly established himself as an expert on prison affairs and was subsequently called on to give evidence to parliamentary enquiries.

Hamilton took a generally more enlightened approach towards Victorian Britain's draconian penal system. He favoured more of a balance between punishment and rehabilitation, but was nevertheless a man of his time – a disciplinarian who embraced 'Victorian Values' and a man with little sympathy for vagrants or habitual criminals.

Yet his mission did not end at the prison gates. He supported charitable causes such as the 'Society for the Protection of Females' and as well as setting up a refuge in the city for released female prisoners, he also helped them find suitably respectable work.

This led him to be instrumental in establishing the penitentiary building on high ground behind Gilesgate, overlooking the river. A contemporary engraving by Joseph Bouet shows the reformatory standing in pleasant open land with smoking chimneys, suggesting a warm welcome within. Life inside was not so cosy, however. The regime was strict and female occupants were closely monitored by staff, led by a resident matron who in turn was overseen by the governors, chaplain and an influential ladies committee. Reports and statistics were used to suggest, for example, what caused the inmates to fall from grace. It seems working in pubs and going to dances were among the main culprits!

Because admission (by petition) was voluntary, occupancy levels at the penitentiary were always low. In the twentieth century, the building became known as Kepier House and the site was used as a children's home and then by the university. Work is now well advanced to restore what remains of the original female asylum and build new student accommodation. No doubt the future 'inmates' will have a much more comfortable stay then their unfortunate Victorian predecessors.

Some may think it slightly ironic that the penitentiary stands behind the 'Chains' – a 1950s block of flats. There is no penal connotation, however. Pedestrians on the steep road between Claypath and Gilesgate were once provided with posts and chains to hang onto in icy weather.

Former penitentiary (with bat nesting boxes).
Inset: Cloister memorial to Hans Hamilton

25. School's Out

A brass nameplate at No. 47 South Street informs us that this is 'Sangreal House'. It is an unusual, even exotic, name – perhaps a former resident's cherished holiday destination? The truth is more home-grown and the fascinating story of Sangreal has lessons for us all.

Education is woven into the history of Durham. In the thirteenth century, novice monks took lessons in the cathedral cloister and the best of them progressed to Oxford University. Learning spread beyond the monastery walls around a century later with the establishment of the Almoner's School for the poor and also the renowned choristers' song school, which continues to this day.

Some of Durham's secular schools became just as well known. Late medieval buildings around Palace Green housed the grammar school which, in 1844, transferred 'over the water' to Quarryheads Lane. There, as Durham School, its reputation continues to grow.

But above all, Durham became a university town. After a false start during Cromwell's Protectorate, Durham University was established in July 1832. A handful of undergraduates began work in what was then a rundown archdeacon's inn (now called Cosin's Hall) on Palace Green. Almost two centuries later, leading churchmen Bishop Van Mildert and Canon Charles Thorp, who proposed it all, would have been astounded to see a university of around 15,000 students spread over and beyond the peninsula.

A far smaller school had a less well-known founder. William Norman Illingworth arrived in Durham's classrooms in 1932 after studying in Leeds and teaching there and in Liverpool, where he was a history master.

Until 1947 he was headmaster of Durham City's Senior School at Whinney Hill before resigning and opening a private school in his home on South Street. 'Sangreal' was very different from Illingworth's earlier schools because of his distinctive educational views. Unlike most others at that time of large classes and regimented learning methods, Sangreal School focused on nurturing the individual creativity, imagination and spirit of its limited number of pupils. Influenced by the ideas of Austrian writer and philosopher Rudolf Steiner, Mr Illingworth's school for boys sought to educate by inspiring 'the feelings and the will instead of reaching merely the intellect'.

A traditional syllabus of science, maths and history (and its public examinations) was not ignored, but Mr Illingworth's believed that those subjects could be taught in a way 'to arouse wonder' and connect them 'to the heart of man'. At No. 47 South Street, living rooms became classrooms that echoed with poetry and song or fell silent with meditation. Painting, drawing and drama were encouraged and the school had a science laboratory which served, among other things, as a theatre and art gallery. Facing the cathedral's west front across the river is a bay window on the second floor. This was the library where each morning, at 9 a.m., the blue-jacketed boys shook hands with Mr Illingworth and his few assistants before starting prayers as the cathedral bell chimed out.

67

According to Illingworth's charming and witty history of his school, published by friends and colleagues after his death in 1980, Sangreal's name was derived from Sir Thomas Malory's *Morte d'Arthur*, first printed by William Caxton in 1485. In this classic translation from the French, King Arthur and his knights pursued the legendary 'Sangreal' or Holy Grail. The remarkable William Illingworth sought his own Holy Grail at Sangreal School, where he taught boys to 'begin to be true men'.

Although Sangreal School closed in 1971, its name endures on South Street. A covenant ensures that this Georgian building will always be known as Sangreal House. Old school days are also remembered in Bishop Cosin's old grammar school (now Divinity House) at the southwest corner of Palace Green. Peering down from the east window are two sculptured heads, now weather-beaten beyond recognition. One might have once smiled and the other scowled. One was said to have passed his exams while the other had failed. Panelling around the former school interior (some of it just visible through a side window) has been initialled by generations of bored schoolboys.

Cosin's Grammar School.
Inset: Former schoolboys initialled the panelling.

26. Secret Services

Many of the 'secret' paths in this book lead to the cathedral and leave the city's other churches far behind. They may lack the grandeur and fame of Durham's mother church, but they share the same spiritual core.

Claypath, for instance, immediately outside the city's old north gate of 'Clewerport' or 'Clayport', has more churches than first meets the eye. This broad, curving thoroughfare leading from the marketplace towards Gilesgate formed an unbroken chain of shops and houses until a chunk of the lower part was removed for the city centre road scheme in the 1960s. Yet a tall church spire still dominates the neighbourhood. Impossible to miss, it has something to hide.

What seems now a typically sober and unthreatening Victorian structure conceals a long history of religious protest. Described in 1894 as a 'chaste' piece of architecture, it was built to the designs of local architect and historian Henry Thomas Gradon. It could seat over 500 of Durham's Congregationalist community, claimed in *Whellands Directory* to be 'the oldest dissenting congregation in the city'.

They could trace their roots back to Protestant doctrinal upheaval in the seventeenth century. Claypath's first dissenting (or nonconformist) clergyman to be recorded was Presbyterian Thomas Dixon, who allowed his own property to be used for services in 1672. Following the Act of Toleration sixteen years later, his home was legalised as a place of worship and in 1750 replaced by a fully fledged chapel.

Attendance slumped in the early nineteenth century but the chapel's fortunes were revived by a merger with Durham's newly formed Congregationalist Church. The Claypath chapel was enlarged, but an even bigger building was required and a 'handsome stone edifice in the Decorated style', costing £5,000 in total, was eventually opened in 1886. It was built in front of the chapel, afterwards a Sunday school, which then became masked from view. Another century has passed it by, but this unpretentious place of worship survives. Round-topped windows and antique brickwork can be seen from the passageway outside the church. Inside, the historic chapel has been transformed and linked to the church as part of a tasteful overall restoration designed by Manchester architects OMI and completed in 2013. A thriving congregation of all ages now gather regularly in the renewed hall of this Anglican Evangelical church. Religious differences seem remote on Claypath now. Victorian church and Georgian chapel are united in what is today called 'Christchurch'.

Not far from it, but further up the slope, St Antony's priory is also secreted away. Only yards from Claypath's traffic noise, this modern religious establishment sits unseen in a surprisingly quiet enclave. The site, originally farmland on which stands the former vicarage of St Nicholas', was acquired by the Society of the Sacred Mission in 1985. Distinguished architect Sarah Menin then added a prize-winning octagonal chapel, which was dedicated in 1992. St Antony's is now an ecumenical centre, used for retreat and contemplation, Christian workshops and everyday prayer. St Antony's and spirituality seem to go hand in hand. Even before entering the main house door, the view over Leazes Road to the cathedral is inspirational.

Above left: Claypath Congregationalist Church.

Above right: St Antony's Priory.

Widely different authors and educationalists are remembered on Claypath. A Blue Plaque on No. 56 marks the house of Victorian scientist, writer and teacher James Finley Weir Johnston. His charitable funding helped establish the Durham School which still bears his name. Student accommodation at the corner of Providence Row and Claypath is dedicated to Ruth First, a South African civil rights activist who lectured at the university from 1973 until 1978.

27. Secret Stones

Small marks on large stones can transport you back to the world of Durham's medieval masons. Geologists have estimated that the cathedral, even without its monastic buildings, required over 68,000 tons of building material. Countless individual blocks were cut and shaped for it from 1093 when foundations were laid until 1133 when the structure was largely complete.

Much of the stone was dressed in local quarries then transported by river barge and horse-drawn cart to the building site. There, innovatory techniques were developed to improve the economy and speed of final construction. Dimensions were standardised for some column sections for instance, and fewer templates were used. It was work of genius and skill, created by the cathedral's original master mason-cum-architect and the stone-working teams who hammered out his designs.

Their handiwork overwhelms you in the nave today. This spectacular space balances strength and beauty, with some massive columns made almost delicate by their chiselled ornamentation. The name of the master who planned them may be unrecorded but many of his workmen, to keep an accurate tally and be paid accordingly, scratched their personal 'signatures' into the finished blocks. The marks of over 100 individual masons have been counted in the cathedral, an ambitious building project inspired by the faith and vision of Durham's early Norman bishops, William of St Calais, Ralph Flambard, and Turgot, the cathedral's English prior.

Knowledge of this period's building practice is limited. Masons were bound to a closely knit, even secretive, tradecraft which vigorously protected its skills and wages. But it is known that training could last for seven years, in which apprentice masons became proficient in both wood and stone-working and were taught some of the basic mathematics which underpinned building design.

Equipped with such skills, the journeyman stonemason embarked on a career that could be relatively well paid and secure, given the employment opportunities created by Europe's great age of castle and cathedral construction. Certainly by the early fifteenth century, when evidence is more plentiful, 'ordinary masons' were well-rewarded Durham craftsmen. And if they should rise through the ranks to become a master, the anonymous writer of the 'Rites of Durham' informs us that they received 'garments at Christmas' and 'food and drink ... whenever'.

Yet when construction stopped – interrupted for financial restrictions perhaps or in winter when mortar would not set – cathedral masons displayed their true resourcefulness. Itinerant Durham craftsmen left their marks on Romanesque churches in Scotland, as far north as the Orkney Isles.

Although paid less during the colder months, other masons may have spent their entire careers in Durham. On-site experimentation was common and the danger of structural collapse was not helped by rudimentary lifting gear and scaffolding (leaving putlog holes scattered across the cathedral walls). Yet while serious building mistakes could be disastrous, a more amusing example survives in the nave today. Staring at one of the south transept's chevron-patterned columns can make you dizzy, but it also reveals a mason's carving gone hopelessly wrong.

As their skills increased some masons' marks became more complex and even evolved into family crests. Those at Durham are generally simpler however – variations on hatched lines, arrowheads and crosses. In the cathedral's light and shade, and often among a field of tool scars, they can be difficult to see but are always a joy to discover.

After searching for their marks, it would be satisfying to meet some of the masons themselves. Two carvings at the south end of the Chapel of the Nine Altars are plausibly suggested by Durham antiquarian J. F. Hodgson to portray members of the stone-working fraternity. Both of them have an artisan's protective skullcap tied under the chin. The formidable Reverend Hodgson, vicar at Witton- le-Wear, believed that either or both of these two 'artists' were responsible for the 'design' of the thirteenth-century chapel which surrounds them.

Miscarved Nave Pier.
Inset: Mason's Head.

28. Shopping Days

Secrets and shopping can go hand in hand. And, rather like bargains, secrets are always worth uncovering. There are some to be found in Durham's indoor market just off the main marketplace. Beyond its Tudor-style archway and colourful stalls is a Victorian building which brought a new style of shopping to Durham.

History books differ on the origins of marketing in Durham City. Some state that trading began with markets on Palace Green during the medieval period while another claims this unlikely in what was then a fortified zone. It seems certain however, that today's more central site was in use as a marketplace during Ralph Flambard's episcopacy at the opening of the twelfth century.

City charters of 1179 and 1180 declared Saturday as market day and established three fairs to be held every year. Commerce was stirring in Durham. For centuries, trading continued in the open-air market space, although tollbooths and then a piazza, built in 1780, provided limited cover from the worst of Durham's weather.

But with the quickening of economic activity in the early nineteenth century, combined with the growing local population, conditions in the marketplace worsened. Expansion of mining communities around Durham also attracted more business into the city and trading spilled into the narrow streets surrounding the marketplace. Tempers must have frayed and takings affected as calls for a better market area grew louder.

After considering other sites around the city, the council made plans to transform the existing marketplace. Although deliberations dragged on, by 1850 it was agreed to develop the north-west side of the area, demolishing some of its 'ruinous property' for a new Town Hall and a much-needed indoor market.

It was built on noble ground. A three-storey mansion belonging to the earls of Westmorland had occupied the site since the late Middle Ages. However, after the disastrous Northern Rising of 1569 their property was confiscated, and the grandeur of 'New Place' or the 'Bull's Head' as it was known faded away. Purchased afterwards by a local charity, it was carved up through the centuries and used as a factory, school, workhouse and tenements.

Its replacement continued the utilitarian trend. Designed by London architect Philip Charles Hardwick, the indoor market was slotted around the Town Hall and Guild Hall – its glass and iron framework hardly out of place on any Victorian railway platform. Indeed, the prolific Hardwick, commissioned after completing Durham's adjacent Town Hall in 1850, was renowned for his grandiose Great Hall at Euston Station.

Durham's market hall is far simpler of course, but characteristic touches of Victorian ornamentation are there to be seen, if not always noticed. As Pevsner points out, the cast-iron roof may be 'usual' enough, but notice the classically inspired supporting iron columns and decoratively pierced beams above them. They were made not just for structural necessity but to demonstrate both the designer's taste and the engineering skills of the Newcastle company which fabricated them.

Durham's covered market opened on Saturday 18 December 1851. A brass bell rung at the close of trading now hangs silently on the upper floor. Of that first Saturday, the *Durham Advertiser* reported 'All Durham' had been there. The same claim could be repeated in today's bustling market hall.

Hardwick (who also designed the Market Tavern public house) was faced with a difficult site which fell sharply to the riverbank. His solution was a fortress-like supporting rear wall. View it closely from behind the market in Walkergate – now a quiet back lane. Tiers of former warehouses can also be seen from there, as well as the hoists which supplied them. Within the market, look up at an oriel window, now projecting awkwardly into the Market Hall. Once on the outside of the Town Hall, it was brought in from the cold when the new market was constructed around it.

Market Entrance.
Inset: Market Bell.

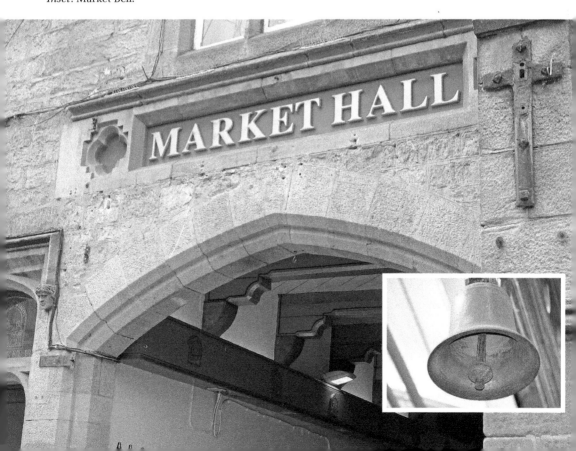

29. Sign of the Cross

Imagine the number of crosses in Durham. Widely seen but often taken for granted, they have historic significance that adds to their Christian symbolism.

St Cuthbert has a cross of his own. The Anglo-Saxon emblem is square or 'pattee' shaped – a design copied from the gold and garneted pectoral cross, which had lain undiscovered in his coffin before it was prised open for the penultimate time in 1827. For those who notice when entering the cathedral, Cuthbert's Cross is encountered immediately on the badges worn by the guides or the bookmarks handed out to visitors.

The real thing – a dainty gleaming jewel – will eventually be exhibited in the dimmed lighting of the cathedral's new 'Open Treasure' display. Cuthbert's Banner however, hanging above the south aisle entrance to the saint's shrine, may attract less attention but glows in its own way. Sponsored fittingly by a Mr John Cuthbert, and embroidered in 'goldwork', the banner was produced by textile artist Ruth O'Leary and other local craftspeople and presented to the cathedral in 2012. Emblazoned with Cuthbert's now iconic cross, this banner is a modern interpretation of an ancient artefact.

Cuthbert's original banner fluttered over English battlefields. According to Victorian antiquarian Hylton Longstaffe, chroniclers first record its existence in 1098 and for several centuries afterwards the legendary flag was marched to war by contingents of Durham men. Reputed to turn defeat into victory (and to be fireproof), the banner was claimed to aid the English triumph at Neville's Cross in 1346. Sadly, the flag's alleged power was no protection against the French wife of William Whittingham, Dean of Durham between 1563 and 1579, who burnt it on her fire.

We can't then be absolutely sure what form the cross on Cuthbert's ancient standard took, or indeed if it was always red (black and yellow are also associated with him). Yet numerous medieval crosses or 'roods' certainly did once surround the saint's tomb. According to the 'Rites of Durham', some of these sacred relics and precious offerings were displayed on red-varnished panelling with gilded lead stars fixed high on the south aisle 'adjoyning to the pillar next St Cuthbert's Feretorie'. Scotland's own fabled cross, the 'Black Rood', was said to be among them, but this is now dismissed. Much so-called 'idolatry' like this was destroyed or stolen in the Dissolution of course, but the coloured splash of Cuthbert's new banner and purposeful old notches in the pillars near it are reminders of vanished medieval wonders.

And there are just as many outside the cathedral. The city has many lost crosses that are believed to have served variously as boundary markers and gathering places, plague crosses or stages on the pilgrim's route. One of the most imposing was the seventeenth-century Market Cross. It featured a sundial but was then demolished and recycled into later market buildings. There were crosses at Framwellgate and Claypath and one at the top of Hallgarth Street called Phillipson's Cross.

Yet among the lost, two crosses can still be found. Hardly recognisable now, the tiny stump of Charley's Cross seems to only fully emerge in winter. In other seasons it is well hidden under the hedgerow from Quarryheads Lane into Church Street. Now listed, this diminutive monument appears to have been named because of its proximity to the fifteenth-century Charlay Close. Much easier to see and once the grandest of all, Neville's Cross, now standing near the busy Darlington Road, is no secret. But stare through its railed enclosure and decide if crumbling figures on the base could be symbols of the four evangelists.

Cuthbert Banner.

DLI Cross.

The cathedral's Durham Light Infantry chapel has the most poignant cross of all. Dedicated in 1924, it contains a simple wooden cross repatriated from the Somme battlefields. It was made by DLI Captain Robert Mauchlen MC, a Newcastle architect who died in 1972. A more unusual cross is often passed by in the North Bailey next to St Mary-le-Bow. The centrepiece of a dedication tablet, this heavily stylised, almost cubist cross is the emblem of St Chad's and commemorates the opening of the college dining hall in 1960. The letters A M D G stand for 'Ad Majorem Dei Gloriam' – 'To the Greater Glory of God.'

30. Take a Letter

Invented around 1700, the humble letter box is now commonplace and instantly recognised. The name of its characteristic shape is given to everything oblong and most doors have at least one ready to receive the mail. But even if today's postmen knew the whereabouts of what must be Durham's most peculiar 'letter box', they would need a ladder to reach it.

High on a side wall of the Grove, at the northern corner of Quarryheads Road, is a little wooden door. Although impossibly far off the ground, it looks like one of the north-east's ubiquitous coal hatches. It is described by a historian of Durham School (which now owns the Grove) as a 'small lock fast cupboard', but it's also a small window into Durham and Britain's postal history.

Although royal and private mail was carried by messengers long before then, the first recognised public postal service began in 1635 with the establishment of a 'Letter Office of England and Scotland'. Legislation for maintenance of the few existing (and largely deplorable) Tudor post roads, on which Durham City was already an important 'post station', was also enacted at this time. At first, 'post boys' on horseback and then stagecoaches and smaller carriages known as 'post chaises' travelled along the Great North Road to Durham.

Communication between England and Scotland became more important after the Act of Union in 1707 helped to increase traffic on this ancient route. Its twenty-first-century successor now flashes past the City of Durham well to the east, but then it went much closer to its heart.

The first maps of Durham show a surprising direction for Durham City's first Great North Road. Published in 1598 and 1610, they suggest that South Street was a major route and the strip map in 'Britannia Depicta' of 1720 confirms its place on the north–south link. This western route was more direct, allowing mail coaches to avoid the city's narrow bridges and streets, and they would also pass closely by the 'cupboard' at the top of South Street.

Without leaving his seat, the coach guard could then deliver letters and packets through the trapdoor or receive outgoing mail. An antique print from the Postal Museum Archive portrays a similar arrangement on the early morning Bath to London run. In this case, the horses hardly break stride as mail pouches are handed over from a second-floor post-house. It was a successful principle which saved time and even survived the coaching age. Years later, mailbags were mechanically retrieved and pushed out by steam trains at high speed. Yet the Grove's postbox days were over even before the railway arrived. By the early nineteenth century, the gentler slope of Elvet's Church Street on the peninsula's eastern flank was the favoured route through Durham. South Street's short-lived 'former glory' as part of the Great North Road would never return.

The late eighteenth and early nineteenth century was a period of great change for the British Post Office; the organisation began to grow up. Improved mail coaches became 'flying machines' and 'postboys' became uniformed 'postmen'. Durham's makeshift postbox at the Grove was forgotten, particularly after 1853 when pillar boxes began to appear on British streets. Not as quintessentially English as they seem however, they were a French or German idea, borrowed by Anthony Trollope, Post Office Surveyor and celebrated author. Sadly, Palace Green's pristine red example is also not original; it's a modern reproduction of a hexagonal 'Penfold' model, first designed in 1866.

Above left: Cupboard on Quarry Heads Lane.

Above right: Market Place flats.

They may be the poor relation of street furniture, but notice the round-headed door next to the indoor market – it has four letterboxes. The alphabetical letters indicate flats which that part of the old building has been converted to. More perplexing is a letter box built into a brick wall behind shops on Elvet Bridge. No doubt intended to be extra secure, it is now disused but was part of the premises of jewellers Blacklock and Son. It is found on what was 'Jailers Yard' – a winding lane that led to the old House of Correction.

31. Take a Seat

Guided tours of the cathedral always spend time telling the story of Bishop Hatfield's imposing fourteenth-century tomb. And so they should. This famous monument on the choir's south side is heavy with blatant symbolism. Built for Thomas Hatfield in his own lifetime, it is surmounted with a bishop's throne – the 'cathedra'– deliberately intended to be even higher than the Pope's in Rome. Seats of all kinds are such commonplace necessities of course, rarely given a thought, but there are some others in Durham which though not so high and mighty as the Prince Bishop's, still have their own tales to tell.

'Count' Boruwlaski's chair in Durham's old Town Hall for instance, sits a little further down the aristocratic scale. Born Joseph Boruwlaski in 1739 and mentioned in chapter 16, this small and genial man settled in Durham in the late eighteenth century after years of touring around various European court circles. Well-read and a gifted musician, he became a local celebrity who was feted by the city's upper crust and followed around the marketplace by inquisitive pitmen fascinated by the nattily dressed little gent. Durham seems to have never forgotten him, and one of his child-sized tailored suits and top hats is preserved in a display cabinet in the Town Hall. His beloved violin stands next to it and both rest on a miniature wicker chair, one of several made for the little 'Count' who, debatably, actually never was.

Yet Durham's original civic buildings in the marketplace once housed a larger seat. For many years, 'chairing the member' was customary after the result of parliamentary elections was declared. To celebrate his victory, the winning candidate was paraded through the streets on a chair which was afterwards stored in the Guildhall. As the often unruly ceremony was dying out by the 1850s however, it's not surprising that no one seems to know what happened to this special chair. It would make an amusing contrast with its tiny companion.

A sedan chair has survived in Durham, however. On display in the North Bailey Heritage Centre, it was used in the nineteenth century by Durham School. Known as the 'Death Chair', it transported sick boys to the school sanatorium – apparently a one-way trip.

And today's Market Place has its own 'special seats'. Recently, this historic public space has become something of a battleground. Lord Londonderry has galloped around the plaza on his electroplated charger and the sea god Neptune has been brought home and similarly shifted about. Paving has been replaced and granite benches now add to the controversial stylistic mix. These granite 'pods' are scattered around the Market Place, as much minimalistic art as the seats they are intended to be.

But they also help to close this historical loop, which, as so often, ends in Durham Cathedral. There, against the north wall opposite the choir, is the last remnant of Bishop Skirlaw's fifteenth-century chantry chapel. Walter Skirlaw was the twenty-fifth prince bishop, a lowly Durham monk who remained modest and generous even after scaling the ecclesiastical heights. All that survives of his fifteenth-century chapel is called the 'Bedesmen's Bench', used as seating long before the installation of pews and now associated with the maroon-robed Bedesmen. For more than 400 years these valuable servants of the cathedral (now lay men and women) have patrolled the aisles, dispensing advice to visitors and aiding the smooth running of Durham's greatest building.

Anyone can now rest on their humble stone bench. It's quieter than the Market Place and a welcome place to sit down and watch another sort of world go by.

Look carefully at the line of heraldic shields set into the base of the Bedesmen's Bench. They are the arms of Bishop Skirlaw and their interwoven pattern of crosses or 'wattles' demonstrates how proud he was of his artisan roots (his family were basket weavers). In the Market Place, more modern craftsmanship is often obscured and difficult to fully appreciate. Scottish artist Ailsa Magnus created the 'Timeline' illustrating key moments in Durham's history. Made from granite, it has bronze insets and is 40 metres long.

Neptune and St Nicholas.

Hatfield's Throne.

32. 'The Play's the Thing'
(*Hamlet* – Act 2)

For such a relatively small place, Durham enjoys a thriving cultural life. Much of this is now symbolised by the Gala Theatre, a multimillion-pound construction opened in 2002 and acclaimed as Durham's new cultural heart. But what of the old heart which still beats in the city's smaller and less eye-catching venues? And what about Durham's long history of entertainment which led to today's gleaming white box of a building in Millennium Square?

Durham's first theatre was set up in 1722 near what appropriately became known as Drury Lane. During this period, artists and musicians were making their homes among Durham's fashionable society and high-class functions were held in the North Bailey's Assembly Rooms. But the popular appeal of Georgian theatre was also evident and by the mid-eighteenth century, a new playhouse occupied an elongated plot off Saddler Street, with an auditorium and stage ranged down the riverside slope.

Cockfighting was part of the neighbourhood's crowd-pulling attractions, and in 1771 a new venue was built on the constricted site. Its success led to the final phase of Durham's mini theatreland when, in 1792, performances began on the opposite side of Saddler Street in another playhouse, parts of which lasted well into the twentieth century. All is now gone, apart from the names of Drury Lane and the occasionally boisterous atmosphere of the nearby Shakespeare pub (what else could it have been called?). But step down through Drury Lane's darkened vennel and 'it's behind you'. Prominent among the cluster of buildings perched above – newer additions grafted onto the old – are the renovated rear elevations of Nos 43 and 44 Saddler Street. Clearly on show is a Georgian period house with Gothic-style windowpanes, a faint reflection of lively times.

Fire damage in 1869 led to the terminal decline of Saddler Street's last theatre. Yet afterwards, city stagecraft was kept alive in Mr Rushworth's North Bailey Rooms, Durham's 'more prestigious place of entertainment'. Like many others, its live performances gradually gave way to film, but this splendid building has been reclaimed as a working theatre, even if it is largely anonymous amid the Bailey's fussier street façades.

Student productions have now replaced shows like the Burgess Minstrels in 1896 and the *Great Train Robbery* in 1903, which may have been the first film drama to be screened in Durham. Recently refurbished, and with seating for over 200, it is another Durham jewel with well-concealed charms. Be prepared to be surprised, for beyond a plain exterior waits a traditional proscenium arch theatre with fine ceilings and plasterwork suggesting a more formal and genteel past.

Most secret of all Durham venues however, is the City Theatre in Fowler's Yard, named after a former business owner. Reach it via another delightfully half-hidden vennel from Silver Street. Or, from the back of St Nicholas church in the marketplace, follow in the footsteps of a medieval archbishop who ran there to escape angry monks. Converted stables and warehouses in old Walkergate are now home to Durham's tiniest playhouse. With only seventy-one seats, actors and audiences are brought closer together, surely the essence of Durham's original theatreland.

Perhaps this brief tour of Durham's playland has now come full circle. After leaving the most little-known theatre, what is now the best known and boldest newcomer is only a short walk away.

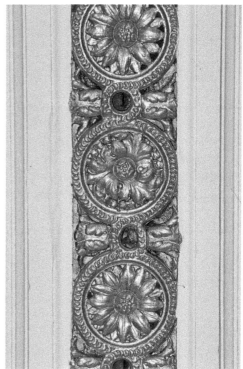

Above left: North Bailey Old Assembly Rooms.

Above right: The auditorium ceiling in the Assembly Rooms.

The Assembly Rooms' art deco façade is the latest of several facelifts since the eighteenth century. Sharp lines and squared 'Crittal'-pattern metal window frames give it a characteristic 1930s' look. It was far too newfangled for local historian Frank Rushford in 1946, and a few years later, Nikolaus Pevsner walked past it without comment.

33. The Prince and the Pitman

A strained neck can be an occupational hazard in Durham Cathedral. Its amazing height tempts you to look upwards, particularly in the majestic crossing. After gazing into the 155-foot lantern tower, turn to the south transept wall so as not to miss the more down-to-earth Haswell Banner.

This large silk flag is a reminder of Durham's rich mining heritage and the connections between the cathedral and the region's former coal-mining communities. Although scaled down over recent years, the annual Miners' Gala continues to be the city's most vibrant celebration. At one of the pageant's most poignant moments, individual pit banners are paraded through Palace Green before being proudly carried into a packed cathedral.

Haswell's dark-blue banner was made in 1893 and the mine closed shortly afterwards. On permanent display since 1989, and said to be the only trade union example in any cathedral, its focus for me has always been the distinctive figure of Tommy Ramsey. Portrayed as usual with his rattle or 'crake', and dressed in top hat and slightly crumpled frock coat, 'Old Tommy' is a folk hero of Durham's early trade union movement. During the long and hard-fought establishment of the Durham Miners' Association, he worked tirelessly, tramping around Durham's pit villages and distributing handbills to promote the cause. He paid the price of his preaching however, relying on handouts after coal owners blacklisted him and their bullyboys roughed him up. Nevertheless, he was eventually triumphant and was appointed a full-time official of the association in 1870, addressing the inaugural Miners Gala in the following year.

Tommy Ramsey died in 1873, careworn beyond his sixty-one years. Despite its own relatively short life however, Haswell Colliery suffered even greater hardships than him. Many lives were lost there, including ninety-five in the explosion of 1844. Only two of the workforce survived. Ramsey would have certainly respected the memory of the dead, but his reaction to the man now portrayed beneath his feet may have been less enthusiastic.

In all the years looking at 'Tommy's Banner', I've hardly noticed the memorial below it or considered the man it commemorates. Sculpted in austere white marble, and looking every inch a lord, the clergyman at prayer is Shute Barrington, the penultimate prince bishop. Born in 1734 and Eton educated, he was destined for high office like his brother, Viscount Barrington – the unfortunate Secretary for War during Britain's loss of its North American colonies. Shute Barrington's Durham career began in 1791 at a time when the prince bishop's power may have been diminished, but his wealth remained considerable.

As north-east industry prospered, income from church lands helped swell the bishop's purse. Some of his clergy were known as 'Golden Canons' and Stanhope in Weardale, the 'richest living in England', was the golden goose. It was surrounded by the Bishop's Park, jealously protected as hunting ground since Norman times. Barrington stepped in to guard its sporting privileges from poachers in 1818, but his bailiffs were well beaten in the resulting scuffle with local unemployed lead miners. For them, he was the 'Fat Man of Auckland and Durham', an insult not helped by the violent intervention of his agents in an earlier coal-mining dispute. Nevertheless, Barrington's typically authoritarian stance was matched by his patronage of education and the arts, religious tolerance and anti-slavery views.

Yet above all, two widely different characters emerge from this slice of history on the cathedral wall. Poles apart in life, they have been brought closer after death.

Ramsey is accompanied on the banner by William Crawford and Scotsman Alex Macdonald, prominent union leaders. Their images are painted and not embroidered as sometimes thought. Although banners were expected to last only around twenty years, Haswell's was rarely used, and after recent skilled conservation, remains in good condition. Barrington's monument, sculpted by society artist Sir Francis Leggat Chantrey, requires little more than occasional dusting. Another mining memorial is nearby. It was built from recycled Spanish and English woodwork, some of it from Bishop Cosin's choir screen, removed during Victorian renovations. Designed by architect Donald McIntyre, the dark-oak construction was placed on the south aisle in 1947 and the book of remembrance, gifted by Vaux Breweries, was added later. Tommy's 'Crake' is now kept in what is known as the 'Stalin' room of the Miners' Hall at Redhills.

Barrington.
Inset: Tommy's Crake.

34. Up and Down

Geography is at Durham's core. Its earliest name, 'Dunholme', was inspired by a striking landscape of rock and river, where 'dun' was the hill and 'holme' the island that it resembled. Medieval authors even compared it to Jerusalem, which like some other fabled cities, was said to be built on seven hills.

Numbering them is debatable now, but Durham certainly remains a city of slopes. They rise and fall to give tempting glimpses of the streets ahead. It follows then that steps and stairways are frequently encountered. Most will not delay you, but a few may stop you in their historic tracks.

After ascending a dog-legged flight of steps at the west end of Elvet Bridge, a wider set is just ahead. Straddling the gap between different street levels at the junction with Saddler Street are the puzzlingly named Magdalene Steps. The area was known as Bailes Corner after a shoemaker's shop, though as Henry Gradon pointed out in 1883, because there used to be two chapels on the bridge (St James and St Andrew), as well as one already dedicated to St Mary Magdalene near Gilesgate, the possibility of another Magdalene or 'Maudlin' chapel here is 'very improbable'. Durham watchers Gibby and Colgrave were nearer the mark half a century later when stating there was a 'Maudlingyld House' nearby in North Bailey.

After Magdalene's quite low steps, stairs in the cathedral rise to almost heavenly heights. Soaring 200 feet with over 300 steps, the winding staircases of the nave's famous Central Tower are worth climbing, although the strenuous privilege must be paid for. While pausing for breath, look out for sections of exposed timber shuttering, left by the cathedral's first builders.

Other long cathedral stairways are well out of public bounds. Rising unseen in their rectangular turrets, they are spiral connections to the maze of galleries and passageways above. Malcolm Thurlby comments that their uncommonly wide treads are more at home in castle keeps than places of worship. Perhaps this adds more weight to Walter Scott's perception of Durham Cathedral as 'Half Church of God – Half Castle 'Gainst the Scot'.

New research also highlights that the spiral or newel stair enhanced the status of their wealthy patrons, but important as they were, their relevance declined in late medieval times. A focus was shifting to domestic interiors where the recognisably modern staircase, 'open and airy', began to appear. Durham has over thirty historic survivors, most constructed from soft-wood deal boards – usually pine – which, as English oak became scarcer, began to be imported from Baltic forests.

Best known among these is Bishop Cosin's 'Black Stairs' in Durham Castle. Constructed in the 1660s, this oak and limewood staircase began to list shortly after it was installed. Shoring up with columns prevented complete collapse, but walking on it now is like crossing a ship's deck at sea. Nevertheless, the Cosin era's exuberant woodcarving exerted considerable influence. Durham's Restoration gentry (and aspiring tradesmen) thought fine staircases would add gravity and style to their townhouses. Unfortunately, most of the remaining examples are privately owned and must stay undisturbed. But the church of St Mary-le-Bow in the North Bailey, now a museum, has a flavour of their lost grandeur. On display is a fragment from what was a splendid seventeenth-century staircase. It graced Lyon's Café on Silver Street, which was Mayor John Duck's Durham mansion, centuries before it was demolished in 1963.

And steps can be even more than essential architectural features. Durham School's 1920s' Gothic-style chapel has ninety-eight of them – one for each of the school's First World War dead.

Magdelene Steps.

Cathedral Spiral Stairway.

A staircase inside Durham School was known to its early schoolboys as 'Hell'. Heaven may be reached at the top of the cathedral's central tower, but rarely in the company of Durham undergraduates perhaps. They are claimed to consider it bad luck before graduation. Some years ago, to guard against suicide attempts, the tower was closed during exam times.

35. Valley of Secrets

Although just a mile to the north-west of the city centre, Durham's Flass Vale is in a different world. Extraordinarily quiet and secluded, the vale is as rich in history as it is in woodland and wildlife. Now mostly culverted, the Flass Burn (formerly the Millburn) flows through this ancient glacial ravine and its boggy evolution is betrayed by a remaining patch of central wetland. Indeed, the term 'Flass' derives from the Scandinavian for 'marsh'.

Today's Flass Vale is the result of change over countless centuries and though now peaceful, has been fought over in the past. Human settlement of the area began around 3,000 years ago as the forested landscape began to be cleared and parts of the vale were probably used for pasture. Livestock grazed over its rough grassland until a few decades ago. Yet long before then, the steep-sided valley had another purpose.

A footpath into the vale from Waddington Street leads to Maiden's Bower, a prehistoric burial mound. Its fairy-tale name probably has more mundane origins, however. Among numerous explanations is that it may simply refer to a cow 'byre' or cowshed and the 'midden' or dunghill associated with it. Maiden's Bowers are scattered over Britain's historical map; there was another on high ground to the east of the city. Durham's second Maiden's Bower (or Arbour) was at the junction of Sunderland Road and Sherburn Road in Gilesgate. Now covered by shops and houses, this obscure antiquity is reputed to have been used for archery practice and long before then to signal across the river to the Iron Age hill fort of Maiden Castle – yet another of Durham's ancient places now veiled in secrecy.

But when first built, Flass Vale's Bronze Age tumulus was intended to be seen. Set on top of a small natural hill, this ancestral burial plot would have been a focus of attention in the once less wooded vale, visible from many points. Long after its purpose was forgotten, the barrow must have retained some significance for local people, woven into their folklore like the roughened tracks which crossed Flass Vale. Yet what may have been a fading memory was given new impetus by the Battle of Neville's Cross in October 1346.

While the precise location of Durham's great Anglo-Scottish fight is uncertain, there is little doubt that battle raged round Crossgate Moor and the Flass valley below it. Medieval chronicles, some more reliable than others, contain accounts of the battle, but only the Rites of Durham makes reference to the 'maydes bower'.

It relates that monks left the relative safety of the cathedral to pray on the small hill during the battle. Carrying a relic of St Cuthbert, they were protected from the mayhem and afterwards a 6-foot-high 'faire crosse of wood' was erected on top of the hillock. Expert opinion doubts much of this colourful 'local tale', but its fascination endures and has helped preserve Flass Vale's identity as a very special place.

Fighting broke out again in more recent times. In 1973, locals combined to resist housing developments nibbling into Flass Vale. Thankfully bloodless this time, the conflict resulted in Flass Vale being declared a Local Wildlife Site in 1982, followed by Local Nature Reserve status in 2008.

Thanks to local voluntary groups, Flass Vale is now a well-managed and thriving area of broadleaved wood in which kingfishers and the occasional deer are seen. So close to the city and yet so far away, it is a secret which deserves to be kept.

The view of the cathedral from Flass Vale.

Flass Burn culvert.

Flass Vale had other secret lives. In Victorian times, it was a recreation spot with paths leading through gardens and orchards to the Rose Tree pub (now a modern hotel). Winter sports were also catered for and in freezing weather the burn was dammed to make a curling pond. Industry also once reached into the vale. With a helping hand from the 'Friends of Flass Vale' however, nature has reclaimed old pits used to extract sand for building. Flass Vale had a darker side as well. A scenic hill on the eastern side was once the macabre Gibbet's Knowle, where corpses of criminals executed nearby were left to rot.

36. Water Walks

Robert Dodsley is another one of Durham's best-kept secrets. He is better known in Nottinghamshire, where he was born in 1703 before moving on to play a significant role in a golden age of British literature. A friend of Defoe, Johnson and Pope, he was an important publisher as well as a bookseller and respected man of letters in his own right. His friendship with cathedral prebend Joseph Spence brought him to Durham in later life and he died there in 1764.

Like so many others, Dodsley was charmed by Durham. For him, the city was 'one of the most romantic places' he knew and the riverbanks were a particular favourite. They were becoming a place to be seen and to take the air. Their development followed the example of the cathedral authorities who, a century before, converted areas around the castle and the town's crumbling walls into their own pleasure gardens and promenades. Sections of Prebends' Walk, for example a raised platform south of the cathedral, are now incorporated within boundary walls which today rarely merit a thought. Gentlemen clerics would once have paraded above your head, taking advantage of fine views across the river gorge. No doubt they enjoyed their elevated position.

Riverside tree cover was increasing in Dodsley's time, yet the peninsula itself was still relatively clear. A mid-eighteenth-century panorama shows the riverbank still laid bare directly below the castle walls – 'the Bishop's Waste' – but with a neat grid pattern of plots over slopes further to the south-east. Owned by affluent Bailey residents, these formal terraces were Durham's own 'hanging gardens', created when the gentry were developing a taste for picturesque landscapes and decorative ruins. Durham's worthies followed the trend, making openings in redundant town walls and ornamenting their gardens with fanciful buildings. Decades of woodland growth have transformed the riverbanks since then – they are wilder now, but as romantic as ever. Yet signs of their polite origins lie half-hidden among the tangled undergrowth.

This secret landscape is for the more adventurous however, and best looked into from the vantage point of the Watergate, rather than explored. Narrow tracks hang below overgrown fragments of medieval town walls along the edge of South Bailey. An ancient tower guards what are now the grounds of St John's College and from there runs Principal's Walk, another exclusive pathway. Below, by Prebends' Bridge on firmer ground, stands the so-called Count's House, a garden folly or extravagant gardener's cottage maybe, but never lived in by Boruwlaski. The Shipperdson family once owned this impressive little temple and behind it is their icehouse, less frequently visited and far less photogenic. Resembling an Egyptian burial chamber, its gloomy entrance is worth scrambling up the slope to peer into.

The opposite bank of the Wear conceals even older secrets. Foliage can be just as dense here, much of it plugging the gaps left by quarries which provided Durham's building stone for centuries. They are recalled by the name of Quarryheads Lane, which follows the river's curve to the south. Further on, between Prebends' Bridge and St Oswald's churchyard, is the now silent Dell which once echoed to the stonebreakers hammer. These old workings, now a flower-filled bowl, were once the 'Sacrist's Quarry'.

Return to Dodsley's grave in front of the cathedral and make what you can of his weathered epitaph (composed probably by Spence). On it Dodsley is described as having 'uncommon industry and merit'. After reading it, you might then plan another of what he fondly called his 'water walks'.

Above left: River Walk at Bow Banks.

Above right: Dodsley Grave.

The Shipperdson icehouse is one of several on the riverbanks. Stocked with winter ice, they supplied the town house kitchens above them for most of the year. Although plans to feature them in a revival of the hanging gardens have not yet fully materialised, this doesn't spoil the walk to Elvet Bridge. Near its arches a fading plaque informs us that this section of pathway from Bow Lane was financed by Dr Andrewes Fearon, a Winchester man (and keen rower) who was headmaster of Durham School between 1882 and 1884.

37. Where's the Whale?

In November 2015, a whale was seen in the River Wear at Durham. One of the highlights of the city's 'Lumiere' festival, the giant sea creature rising from the dark water near Elvet Bridge was a 3D projection created by French artist Catherine Garret. It was not the first whale to come to Durham. In 1767 the bones of a sperm whale were carted through Durham's streets. They were on their way to the castle where the bishop accepted the remains of this 'royal fish'. Whales, porpoises and sturgeon were included in this category and in the early fourteenth century were deemed to be Crown property when caught in English waters or found stranded on its shores.

In practice however, local nobility and ecclesiastical authorities were also known to lay claim to this valuable commodity, although the whale's head and tail were usually returned to the monarch. But it was as the king's representative that Durham's prince bishops insisted on their own exclusive right to this rare sea prize.

Unsurprisingly then, Bishop Richard Trevor soon showed an interest in the large whale that floated into his territory. At the end of November 1766, shortly after it was spotted

Lumiere Whale.

near the mouth of the Tees, the dying mammal was beached by the crew of the cargo ship *Nancy*. Work began almost immediately to butcher the carcass and any lingering questions of ownership were resolved by the arrival of John Robson, the bishop's agent.

The unfortunate whale provided over a ton of precious spermaceti and fifty-four casks of blubber were later boiled down for sale on the London whale oil market. It seems that the bishop lost out financially on the deal, but kept the whale skeleton as a 'mark of his regality'.

And so the 50-foot-long specimen came to Durham. After being discarded among rubbish in a castle basement, it was rediscovered in 1839 and eventually displayed for many years in the cathedral undercroft. Some schoolboys believed it was the 'authentic' whale of Jonah fame, but it sunk from view once more in the 1970s when the undercroft was converted for use as a restaurant and treasury.

Hopes were raised that the bones would be on show once more after they were taken to the university, but for now the 'Bishop's Whale' is in the care of Beamish Museum, even further inland from its deep-sea home.

38. Last Look

Like the first, this book's final steps are from the Market Place to the cathedral. It's a short journey never to be tired of and one that still has secrets to give up.

The junction of the Market Place between Silver Street and Saddler Street was popularly known as 'Pulleine Corner' because of the poultry once sold there. But the Market Place is now better known for its sea creatures and gods than birds. Nowadays, seafood and game are sold in the market's indoor hall and outside on his new plinth, Neptune the sea king stands triumphant with his foot on a dolphin's neck and his trident poised to strike.

In fact, he represents the failure of eighteenth-century Durham's seagoing plans. An astonishing river link between the city and the sea was first proposed by wealthy coal owner George Bowes. He presented the statue to Durham in 1729 as a token of his ambition. Although the schemes went nowhere, Neptune travelled far. Sited on top of successive Market Place pants before a long exile in Wharton Park, he was damaged by vehicles and vandals and had to be restored and repaired. Even after 'the Old Man of the Sea' came home in 1991, the lead statue was shuffled around the Market Square and now makes a strange bedfellow with Lord Londonderry and the recently unveiled Korean War infantryman. But beyond this highly visible trio, you must look harder for any birds. There are a few, created by ceramicist Annette Poulson. Small and curious pieces of street furniture, they perch above shopfronts. One of them, over the restaurant which now bends around Pulleine Corner, is a puffin. Is its beak crammed with fish?

Old ceilings and older timber frames lie beneath the skin of Saddler Street, but history also shows on the surface. High on the renovated gable of No. 36, below decorative bargeboards, are carved the initials 'TM' and the date '1844'. At that time, one of the occupants of the premises was house painter Thomas Meggeson. A café now takes his place, its name etched across ground-floor windows. A few doors away, however, behind the corporate sign on Nos 41 and 42, older and more formal 'branding' survives. This 'Mannerist-style' shop has antique charm. From a vividly tiled yet unnoticed threshold, to a back room overlooking historic Drury Lane, the building offers something more than the 'exclusive' fashions on sale today. Climb narrow stairs to an unusual iron-railed gallery to better appreciate the shop's first-floor painted-glass windows. A city crest and scrolls advertise the tailoring work of its Victorian shopkeepers; William Grey and his family supplied university gowns from Saddler Street for over a century.

Vehicles and pedestrians have competed for space in this confined part of Durham for many years. Even in 1724, almost a century before the North Gate was demolished, a carriage owner was fined sixpence for blocking the North Bailey around St Mary-le-Bow. Collision avoidance measures appear to have been adopted, however. Notice chamfered brickwork at the corner of Owengate and at Bow Lane as you turn to approach the cathedral and journey's end.

But before entering, pause outside. Below the Great West Window (the Rose Window) is an elusive, if humble, relic. Now almost invisible, a Latin inscription has been cut into a buttress at the foot of the Chapel of the Nine Altars. Possibly the handiwork of the chapel's master mason, it translates as 'Thomas Moises laid this stone.'

Fortunately, a plaster cast has been taken of this simple dedication. See the real thing before it vanishes forever.

Sometimes Durham Cathedral puts on a strange face. Stand for long enough opposite the North Door with your back to the High Altar and you may see it high above. He (or she?) is just a mirage of course – a trick of the light on a crumpled section of vault plasterwork.

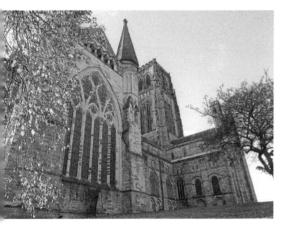 

Above left: Chapel of Nine Altars.

Above right: Saddler Street gable.

Right: Saddler Street mosaic.

Bibliography

Allan, G., *View of the City of Durham* (1824)

Andrews, W., *Bygone Durham* (1898)

Austin, R., *The Rites of Durham* (ND)

Boyle, J., *Guide to Durham*

Brickstock, R., *Durham Castle* (2007)

Butler, D. and C. Wilkes, *The History of Durham Indoor Market* (2000)

Clack, P., *Book of Durham City* (1985)

Colgrave, B. and C. Gibby, *A Short Tour of Durham* (1952)

Gradon, H., *The Ancient City of Durham* (1883)

Green, L., *Building St Cuthbert's Shrine* (2013)

Hugill, R., *Castles of Durham* (1979)

Johnson, M., *Durham* (1991)

Mee, A., *Durham* (1953)

Nixon, P. and D. Dunlop, *Exploring Durham History* (1998)

Pevsner, N., *County Durham* (1990)

Pocock, D., *The Story of Durham* (2013)

Pocock, D. et al., *Durham Cathedral* (2014)

Proud, K., *Durham City* (2003)

Roberts, M., *1000 Years of History* (2011)

Rollason D. and M. Prestwich et al., *The Battle of Neville's Cross* (1998)

Rushford, F., *In and Around Durham* (1946)

Simpson, D., *Durham Millennium* (1995)

Stranks, C., This Sumptuous Church (1993)

Usherwood, P. et al., *Public Sculpture of North East England* (2000)

Webb, S., *In Search of the Little Count* (2008)

Webb, S., *The Prince Bishops of Durham* (2011)

Woodhouse, R., *The Durham Book of Days* (2014)

Archaeologia Aeliana

Durham County Local History Society Bulletins and Journals

Durham Archaeological Journal

Durham Advertiser

Victoria County History

Acknowledgements

I am indebted to many people who have helped me with this book and can only apologise to those not mentioned here. Particular thanks are due to Damon Rogers of 'Trampas' in Owengate, Kacey Courtney at the former Assembly Rooms (now University Theatre), Gemma Lewis at the Castle, Kevin at the Miners' Hall, the Bremner family on Claypath, Keith and Maggie Bell at Crook Hall and staff at the University Library on Palace Green, St Mary-le-Bow Heritage Centre and local studies at Clayport. Once again Andrew drew the maps and June read the proofs. John Hayton provided invaluable source material and further information was contributed by David Butler, Colin Wilkes, Avril Ferry, Jenny Parker, Chris Woods and Norman Emery. Mr Graham Potts, retired Senior Lecturer in History at Sunderland University, kindly commented on the text and suggested helpful additions and improvements. Any remaining faults however are entirely mine. All photographs, excepting those of Jacob Bee's Diary (courtesy of Durham University Library), are by the author.

Photographic compilations by:
June Crosby
Durham Photographic Society
Ian Nelson
Philip Nixon
Michael Richardson

Also Available from Amberley Publishing

MICHAEL RICHARDSON

DURHAM CITY
From Old Photographs

This fascinating selection of photographs traces the history of
Durham City.

Paperback
illustrated
128 pages
978-1-84868-507-9

Available from all good bookshops or to order direct
please call **01453-847-800**
www.amberley-books.com